Smart Choices for Preteen Kids

Loveland, Colorado

Smart Choices for Preteen Kids

Credits
Thanks to all the authors who contributed great lessons to Active Bible Curriculum®.
Compilation Editor: Jim Hawley
Editor: Debbie Gowensmith
Creative Development Editor: Ivy Beckwith
Chief Creative Officer: Joani Schultz
Copy Editor: Helen Turnbull
Art Director: Kari K. Monson
Cover Art Director: Jeff A. Storm
Computer Graphic Artist: Joyce Douglas
Cover Photographer: Jafe Parsons
Illustrator: Gary Templin
Production Manager: Peggy Naylor

Library of Congress Cataloging-in-Publication Data
Smart choices for preteen kids.
        p.   cm.
    ISBN 0-7644-2039-9 (alk. paper)
    1. Christian ethics. 2. Children–Conduct of life. 3. Decision
-making–Religious aspects–Christianity. I. Group Publishing.
BJ1261.S62   1998
248.8'2–dc21   97-44037
                                                                   CIP

10 9 8 7 6 5   07 06 05 04 03 02 01 00

Printed in the United States of America.
Visit our Web site: www.grouppublishing.com

Contents

Introduction

The preteen years are challenging...both for the kids and for you. Ten- to twelve-year-olds often receive mixed messages about whether they're still children or mature young people. Kids this age are starting to develop their independence, so they're questioning authority and tradition more than ever before. They're noticing that the world is full of unfamiliar and exciting possibilities. Add those developmental qualities to our fast-paced, grow-up-soon world, and the preteen years can become a turning point.

Will your kids get through them with a stronger, active faith?

You want your kids to *use* their faith in their new world. You want them to turn to the Bible and God for decision-making help. And you want them to react to their world with good, smart choices.

In *Smart Choices for Preteen Kids,* the active-learning lessons can help your kids prepare for real-world choices. Because these lessons creatively explore issues kids struggle with, the activities will intrigue your kids. They'll be caught up in the learning.

Each lesson addresses an attainable goal that's based on Scripture, so the activities give your kids the solid biblical background they need to make choices. The lessons also encourage kids to do what God wants them to do. They'll walk away from these lessons with a greater understanding of the choices they face, of how their faith influences those choices, of what God wants and why; and they'll be armed with specific responses to those choices.

Because the preteen years can be a turning point, *Smart Choices for Preteen Kids* strives to help you help your kids enter their teenage years with a stronger faith, a better understanding of Scripture, and a commitment to do what God wants them to do. With these active, pertinent, and biblically based lessons, your kids' faith can develop a "growth spurt" that will last the rest of their lives.

Me and My Friends

Goal:
To understand that they were created in God's image.

Scripture Verses:
Genesis 1:26-27; 5:1-2; Matthew 5:1-16

Created in God's Image

Preteens may hear conflicting arguments about the creation of the world from school, parents, and church. But what's *really* important for preteens to know about creation? Kids need to see beyond the controversy to a key ingredient of creation: They were created in God's image.

Opening

Speed Draw

(For this activity, you'll need newsprint, markers, the "Game Words" list in the margin, a sheet of paper, and candy or gum.)

Have kids form teams of no more than five. Have each team find its own place in the room, and then give each team newsprint and markers. Ask one person from each team to come see you. Show each of these people the first word on the "Game Words" list in the margin (cover the rest of the words with a sheet of paper).

Then have each of these people run back to his or her team and silently draw pictures—not letters, numbers, or symbols—depicting the word. When someone in a team guesses the exact word, that person must run to you and tell you the word. Then show that person the next word from the "Game Words" list, and have that person run back to draw pictures. Continue the game until one team has guessed all the words. Give the members of that team a prize of candy or gum. Then ask:

● **What's your reaction to this game?**
● **Was it easy or difficult to guess the words? Explain.**
● **Did the words you guessed seem to be related? Explain.**

Say: **The words in this game were connected by a theme: creation. Just as you tried to figure out the words being drawn, many people try to figure out how they were created. Today we'll explore what's really important for us to know about creation.**

Game Words
Heaven
Light
Life
Create
Multiply
Good
Seas
Image
Breath
Garden

Creation Debate

*(For this activity, you'll need Bibles, a copy of the "Creation Debate"
handout on page 10, scissors, paper, and pencils.)*

Have kids form four teams; then assign an area of the room to each
team. Cut apart the sections of the "Creation Debate" handout (p. 10).
Give each team one section, a Bible, paper, and pencils.

Say: **In your groups, read your section of the handout. This
describes how you'll approach the issue of creation in a debate
we'll start in just a few minutes. Talk about how you'll act in the
debate based on the instructions on your handout.**

Allow four minutes for kids to read and discuss the handout. Then have
kids set up their chairs in one square, with each team creating one side of
the square. First allow each team one minute to present its position; then
tell teams they can challenge things the other teams said. Allow a minute
or two of mayhem, and then call time. Have kids form a circle, and ask:

● **How'd you feel as you presented your position?**

● **How'd you feel when everyone started talking at once?**

● **How'd this activity mirror the way some people approach
the issue of creation?**

● **What did you learn about the creation debate from this activity?**

Say: **Arguing about creation often doesn't accomplish anything.
Instead, we lose sight of the fact that we were created in God's
image.** Ask:

● **How does knowing that you were created in God's image
make you feel?** (Kids may feel uncomfortable answering this question.
If they say things such as "God must look pretty funny" or "I feel sorry
for God," talk about how God sees each person as important and worthwhile—no matter what we see as our faults. Be sensitive to kids who feel
they're ugly or who have difficulty relating to other kids.)

Say: **Being created in God's image means we're like him in
many ways. But we're also different from him. Let's take a look at
some of the similarities and differences.**

The Bible Experience

Same and Different

(For this activity, you'll need Bibles.)

Have kids form groups of no more than three, and give each group a
Bible. In their groups, have kids read Genesis 1:26-27; 5:1-2 and then discuss the following questions:

● How do people differ from animals?

● What does it mean to rule over the animals?

● In what ways are people similar to God?

● How are people different from God?

Have kids get into new groups with different group members and share what they discussed in their first groups. Then ask:

● **What do you think it means to be created in God's image?** (This can be a tough question for kids. You might want to have a pastor talk briefly about your church's approach to this question.)

● **What makes humans unique?**

Have kids read Matthew 5:1-16 and then discuss the following questions:

● **How can we act as children of God in everyday situations?**

● **Will this affect the way you live each day as a Christian? Why or why not?**

Say: **Realizing that we were created in God's image can feel overwhelming, and living as children of God every day can be tough. But each of us is developing qualities that help us live as God wants us to.**

Make a Commitment

Strength Bombardment

(For this activity, you'll need four balls.)

Have kids stand and form a square as they did in chairs for the "Creation Debate" activity. Give one person on each of the four sides of the square a ball. Say: **When you formed this square earlier, you debated about how the world was created. But now as you look around, think about the wonderful purpose God has for each one of you—his creation.**

When I say "go," say one way you see God reflected in a particular person here. For example, you might say, "I see God reflected in you because you're kind to others." Then call out that person's name and toss him or her the ball. Be ready because there are four balls, and they may come to you at any time. Be sure everyone gets tossed a ball at least once. The positive things you say will help build strength in the people you say them about.

Allow three to five minutes for kids to toss the balls and tell ways they see God reflected in each other. Then ask:

● **What can we do differently in our lives to better reflect the image of God in us?**

Have each student tell one thing he or she will do to better reflect God's image.

Sing Praises

(For this activity, you'll need paper, pencils, and hymnals.)

Have kids choose a familiar hymn or song they enjoy singing. Then have kids form groups of no more than four, and have each group write a new verse for that song which describes the wonder of God's creation. Allow five minutes for groups to write their verses. Close by having each group sing its verse of the song.

Creation Debate

Cut apart these four cards, and give one to each team.

Scientific Study Group

Your group doesn't think religion and science mix. You say things such as "Since we can't go back to the beginning of time, there's no way to know what God did or didn't do. The only facts we have are facts we can prove today." You think the Bible is a book of interesting stories but isn't a useful tool for scientific study.

Sum up your position with a statement to convince the other groups that science is the only way to define the origin of the world.

When the time comes to challenge other groups, you should all begin talking at once, trying to convince the other groups that you're right. Try to stir up the other groups by pointing out the holes in their positions.

Divine Design Group

Your group wants others to understand that the importance of the biblical account of creation is the message it brings to Christians. You say things such as "The importance of creation isn't how it happened but why it happened." You don't think creation could've happened by chance, suggesting that God was in charge.

Sum up your position with a statement to convince the other groups that our lives have meaning because of God's plan. Emphasize that whether it took a million years or a day, the important thing to remember is that people were created in God's image.

When the time comes to challenge other groups, you should all begin talking at once, trying to convince the other groups that you're right. Try to stir up the other groups by pointing out the holes in their positions.

Believable Bible Group

Your group wants others to understand that the Bible is an exact record of the beginning of the world. You believe that a "day" in the biblical account of creation is a twenty-four-hour day.

Sum up your position with a statement to convince the other groups that the Bible holds the exact and only truth about creation.

When the time comes to challenge other groups, you should all begin talking at once, trying to convince the other groups that you're right. Try to stir up the other groups by pointing out the holes in their positions.

Concerned Christian Group

Your group believes that science and religion can work together to describe the beginning of the world. You believe it's possible that the world was created as the scientific group describes, but you believe God had a hand in the process.

Sum up your position with a statement to convince the other groups that science only supports the fact that we have a wonderful Creator.

When the time comes to challenge other groups, you should all begin talking at once, trying to convince the other groups that you're right. Try to stir up the other groups by pointing out the holes in their positions.

Doing My Best

Goal:
To give their best to God.

Scripture Verses:
Genesis 4:1-15;
Matthew 6:33

Many people and activities vie for top priority in preteens' lives. Kids may put their relationship with God aside because it just doesn't seem as urgent as other things. Kids need to see the importance of making their relationship with God top priority in their lives.

Opening

What's Best?

(For this activity, you'll need tape, newsprint, and markers.)

Tape five sheets of newsprint to a wall. On each, write one of the following headings: "food," "movie," "free-time activity," "school subject," and "music group or artist."

Give kids markers, and have each person write on each sheet of newsprint one item he or she thinks is the best for that category. For example, someone might write, "chocolate ice cream," "steak," or "spaghetti" on the food list. Then have each person explain his or her choice for each list. Have kids vote on the best item in each category, and circle the winning items. Ask:

● **How easy was it to choose the best item in each category? Explain.**

● **What characteristics help make these things the best?**

● **What goes into making something the best?**

● **What kinds of things do you put your best into?**

Say: **Each of us may have a different opinion about what is the best food or the best movie, and we may put our best efforts into different activities. But God wants our best, too. Today we'll learn how to give God our best.**

Reflection and Application
Second Best?

(For this activity, you'll need plastic straws, marshmallows, and small prizes.)

Have kids form groups of no more than five. Give each group a few plastic straws and marshmallows. Say: **We're going to see who can create the most beautiful sculpture out of marshmallows and straws. These sculptures should represent God's love for us. The winning sculpture will get a special prize.**

Encourage kids to be creative in their sculpting. After about five minutes of sculpting, have groups take turns explaining their sculptures to the rest of the class.

Walk up to one group's sculpture, and say: **This sculpture represents a great amount of effort. A prize goes to this team for its hard work.**

Give the team a prize. Then walk up to another group's sculpture and say the same thing. Give that team a prize, too. Do this for each sculpture. Then ask:

● **How'd you feel when I awarded the first prize?**

● **How'd you feel when I began to award a prize for all the sculptures?**

● **How is giving your best different from being the best?**

● **Was it easy or difficult to give your best effort in this activity? Explain.**

● **How is giving your best effort in this activity like giving your best to God?**

● **How is the result of this activity like the result of giving our best to God?**

Say: **God desires our best. But sometimes we don't feel like giving our best to him—or we don't have the right attitude. Let's look at the story of Cain and Abel to see what God wants from us.**

The Bible Experience
Right Attitude

(For this activity, you'll need a Bible and cookies.)

Have someone read aloud Genesis 4:1-15. Then have kids form groups of no more than five. Have each group briefly discuss the following questions:

● **Why didn't God accept Cain's offering?**

● **Does it seem unfair that God didn't accept Cain's offering? Explain.**

● **Why was Cain upset with God?**

● **Have you ever felt like Cain did after his offering wasn't accepted? Explain.**

● **Based on this passage, how important is it to give God your best effort?**

Have kids form a circle, give each person a cookie, and tell kids not to eat the cookies. Say: **It may seem unfair, but God doesn't want to accept our second-best effort. Just as Abel gave the best sacrifice he had to God, we must give the best we have to offer.**

Imagine for a moment that the cookie I've given each of you represents the best you can give to God. Think about what it means for you to give your best to God. For example, you might think giving your best to God means going to church regularly. In a minute, each of you will come to the front of the room, tell what giving your best to God means to you, and place your cookie on this "altar" (point to a nearby table).

Allow kids a minute to think. Then have each person take a turn saying what giving his or her best to God means and then placing a cookie on the altar. Be sure to include yourself in this activity. When kids have placed their cookies on the altar, collect the cookies and set them aside. Ask:

● **Was it easy to describe what it means to give your best to God? Why or why not?**

● **How'd you feel when I asked you to give up your cookies?**

Say: **Sometimes giving our best to God requires sacrifice. Just as you gave your cookies away, you may have to give up something you like in order to give God your best. For example, if you enjoy spending time with friends but friends are interfering with your relationship with God, you may have to limit your time with friends.**

Have kids call out other ways they might have to sacrifice to give their best to God. Read aloud Matthew 6:33. Then ask:

● **What does it mean to seek God first?**

Say: **In this verse, Jesus speaks about trusting God to take care of us. But the key words in the verse, "seek first," tell us something else about God. He wants our relationship with him to be the focus of our lives. By seeking God first, we'll learn to give him our best. When we place God low on our priority list, we don't give him our best.**

Make a Commitment

Giving Your Best

(For this activity, you'll need copies of the "What I'll Give" handout on page 15, pencils, and cookies.)

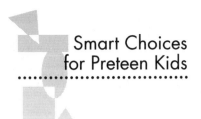

Give each person a "What I'll Give" handout (p. 15) and a pencil; then have kids complete the handout.

Have kids form groups of no more than four to discuss their handouts. Ask each person to share at least one thing they plan to do to give their best to God.

Then ask everyone to form a circle. Say: **Earlier we discovered that giving God our best may require sacrifice. But when we give God our best, we often see rewards come back in surprising ways.**

Go around the circle, and give everyone a cookie. Tell kids that the cookies represent God's response to their willingness to give him their best. As you hand each person a cookie, tell one thing you appreciate about his or her relationship with God. For example, you might say, "I appreciate your willingness to learn more about God" or "I'm glad you're committed to serving God first."

After you've gone around the circle, allow kids to walk around and affirm each other for committing to give God their best.

Closing

Best Prayer

(For this activity, you'll need tape, newsprint, and a marker.)

Tape two sheets of newsprint to a wall. Have kids get into two groups, and then say: **Each group is going to write a prayer to God, asking him to help us give our best to him. In each group, one person at a time should silently come up to the newsprint and write a portion of the prayer. You don't need to say much, but be honest and focus on how we can give God our best.**

Begin the prayers by using a marker to write the same opening to each prayer. Then encourage kids to add words or sentences to the prayer. When each prayer is complete, have everyone gather together; then read each prayer in unison as your closing.

WHAT I'LL GIVE

What does it mean to give God your best? It might mean spending more time in prayer. Or it might mean trusting God to help you overcome temptations. Think about your relationship with God. Then draw a picture to represent this relationship in the space below. What does your picture say about the priority you give your relationship with God?

Complete the following sentences with specific ways you'll give your best to God. For example, for the "school" sentence you might write, "I'll be more open about my relationship with God when I talk with friends."

One way I'll give my best to God while at school is...

One way I'll give my best to God while at home is...

One way I'll give my best to God while at church is...

One way I'll give my best to God every day is...

First Steps: Guy-Girl Friendships

Although preteens generally like to stick with same-sex friendships, some may begin to explore guy-girl friendships—or even boyfriend-girlfriend relationships. These kids will often choose boyfriends or girlfriends on the basis of a few exchanged notes and the encouragement of their friends. Then, for some unknown reason, things just don't work out. Why?

Friendship is the basis of all healthy relationships. Kids need to understand how important friendship is and need to learn to cultivate friendship in their guy-girl relationships.

Opening

Three-Legged Race

(For this activity, you'll need strips of cloth or rope.)

Tell the group that this game requires absolute silence. Have each student find a partner sitting beside him or her. Pass out strips of cloth or rope to each pair, and have them tie two of their legs together—without talking.

Have pairs move to a starting line at one end of the room, and then conduct a quick three-legged race. Tell kids that anyone who talks will be disqualified. Congratulate the winning pair, and then ask:

● **What was difficult about this game?**

● **How would your chances of winning have been better if you could have talked with your partner?**

Say: **Today we'll see how it's difficult to win—whether in a game or in a real-life situation—without being able to communicate as friends.**

16

Time-Travel Troubles

(For this activity, you'll need paper and a marker.)

Have kids remain in their pairs, and give each pair a sheet of paper that has a different activity written on it. Here are several ideas for activities:

- starting a car,
- plugging in and turning on a light,
- making a phone call,
- typing the alphabet,
- making a glass of lemonade with ice in it, or
- riding a bicycle.

Explain that you're a person who has just been transported from thousands of years ago to the present through a strange accident. Say: **In order to get by in the present, I'm going to have to learn how to do some present-day things. I need each pair to explain to me exactly how to do the activity written on the piece of paper.**

Give each pair one or two minutes to explain the activity. Make the activity as difficult as possible for them to explain. For example, if they say, "Get in the car," ask, "What's a car?" For every answer they give, ask another question.

After each pair has attempted an explanation, gather the students together. Ask:

- **How did you feel when you were trying to explain a simple activity to me?**
- **How was this activity like trying to talk to a member of the opposite sex?**
- **Do you think there are some differences between the ways guys and girls communicate? Explain.**

Say: **Sometimes talking to members of the opposite sex is like talking to people from a different time period: They don't seem to understand us, and we don't seem to understand them. But if we don't communicate, things never work out, and both sides become frustrated and confused. One way we can communicate better and build friendships with others is to learn more about others.**

The Bible Experience

Interests Survey

(For this activity, you'll need a Bible, copies of the "Interests Survey" handout on page 19, and pencils.)

Hand out the "Interests Survey" handouts (p. 19) and pencils. Give kids three minutes to fill out as much of the surveys as possible.

Encourage kids to get as many names as possible on their surveys.

After three minutes, gather the group together to see who was able to complete the survey. Ask:

● **Did you find out anything new about someone else in the group? What?**

Read aloud Philippians 2:3-8. Ask:

● **What do you think these verses mean?**

● **How do you feel when people know the things you're interested in but then ignore those things?**

● **How does this Scripture apply to guy-girl relationships?**

● **How do you feel when a friend agrees to do something you enjoy even though it's not his or her favorite activity?**

Say: **When you were trying to communicate with the person from another time period, it was difficult because you didn't have much in common. But now we've found a few things we have in common, and we know it's important to consider others' interests with our own. That's the basis for friendship.**

Make a Commitment
Balloon Brainstorm

(For this activity, you'll need a balloon and a marker.)

Inflate a balloon, and write the word "friendship" on it. Have students sit in a circle and bounce the balloon around. After every few bounces, stop the play and have the person with the balloon tell one specific thing he or she is going to do to build friendships—for example, "I'm going to listen when my friend talks instead of interrupting." After each student has had a turn, say: **From our commitments today, it's easy to see that friendship can be expressed in many different ways. And each of us is uniquely gifted to express friendship to others.**

Closing
My Treat

(For this activity, you'll need candy.)

Give each person a piece of candy. Tell the students that they must each give the treat to another person in the group and tell that person one way his or her friendship is a treat to others. For example, someone might say, "Your friendship is a treat because you're so giving."

When kids are finished, say: **Always remember to "treat" yourself right by building healthy friendships.**

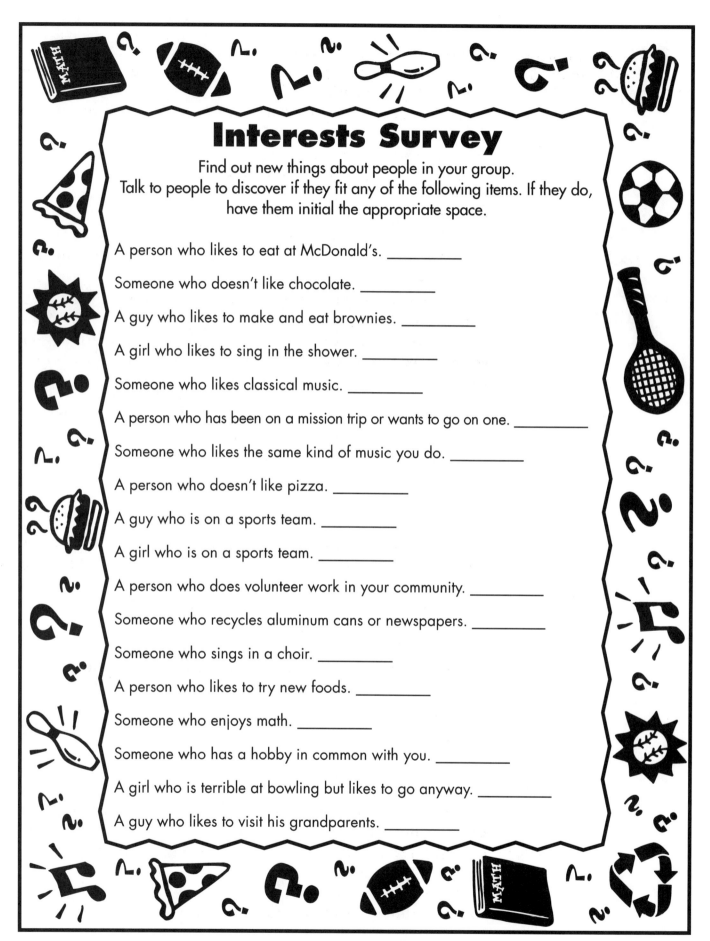

Interests Survey

Find out new things about people in your group.
Talk to people to discover if they fit any of the following items. If they do,
have them initial the appropriate space.

A person who likes to eat at McDonald's. _____

Someone who doesn't like chocolate. _____

A guy who likes to make and eat brownies. _____

A girl who likes to sing in the shower. _____

Someone who likes classical music. _____

A person who has been on a mission trip or wants to go on one. _____

Someone who likes the same kind of music you do. _____

A person who doesn't like pizza. _____

A guy who is on a sports team. _____

A girl who is on a sports team. _____

A person who does volunteer work in your community. _____

Someone who recycles aluminum cans or newspapers. _____

Someone who sings in a choir. _____

A person who likes to try new foods. _____

Someone who enjoys math. _____

Someone who has a hobby in common with you. _____

A girl who is terrible at bowling but likes to go anyway. _____

A guy who likes to visit his grandparents. _____

Forgiving My Friends

"I can't believe she said that to me!"

"I don't know why I ever thought he was my friend!"

Preteens' friendships can be volatile. Some of their friendships last for years, some bottom out after just a few weeks, and some seem to ride a perpetual roller coaster. Despite what your kids may think, there *are* ways to build healthy, fun, lasting friendships—and positive ways to deal with relationships that die.

Opening

Pairs Tag

Have everyone select a partner and link elbows with that person. Have the pairs spread around the room, leaving plenty of room in between to move. Select one pair, and assign one partner to be "It" and the other to be the runner.

Say: **In this game of Tag, the runner may grab the arm of any person standing in the room. When this happens, the runner and the person he or she grabs form a new pair, and the third person then becomes the runner. At any time, if "It" tags the runner, then the runner becomes "It."** To begin the game, call out: **Go!**

After about five minutes, end the game. Then ask:

● **What was fun about this game?**

● **How was this game like your friendships sometimes are?**

Say: **In this game you were forced out of a partnership, and the only way to survive was to form a new partnership. Relationships can be the same way. They always seem to be changing. Today we're going to learn more about our changing relationships.**

Reflection and Application

Friend or Foe?

(For this activity, you'll need blindfolds and Hershey's Kisses candies or another small snack.)

Before the meeting, select two adult leaders or class members, and give them each a stash of Hershey's Kisses candies or another small snack.

Have each person find a partner. In each pair, have the person whose birthday is closest to today put on a blindfold. Then have your two helpers station themselves on opposite sides of the room.

Say: **As a reward for putting on the blindfold, your partner will lead you to a piece of candy. Candy for blindfolded people is located over there** (point to one of your helpers). **However, if those of you who are not blindfolded would rather have candy for yourselves, lead your partners over there** (point to the other helper), **and you'll receive the candy instead. It's up to you.**

Let the seeing students lead their partners to whichever side they've chosen.

Allow everyone to take off their blindfolds; then gather the group together again. Ask:

● **If your partner led you to a piece of candy for yourself, would you choose this person again as a partner? Why or why not?**

● **If your partner led you to a piece of candy for himself or herself, would you choose this person again as a partner? Why or why not?**

● **How did those of you who were leading feel about making the decision? Explain.**

● **How was this activity like real friendships?**

● **How do you feel when you find out a friend has lied, talked behind your back, or done something else that hurts you?**

Say: **We're bound to have problems in our relationships. Some problems may be worth working out, but sometimes it's best to let a relationship end. Let's look at some people in the Bible who had problem relationships.**

The Bible Experience

Bible Soap

(For this activity, you'll need a copy of the "Soap Stories" handout on page 24 and Bibles.)

Have the kids form two groups. Give one group the "As the Stomach Churns" section of the handout (p. 24) and the other group the "One Life to Live or Lose" section. Make sure each group has a Bible.

Say: **Use the information on your handout and in the Bible to learn about a relationship that came to an end. Then transform your story into an episode of a soap opera to perform for the other group. Each person must participate as an actor or a prop.**

Give the groups a few minutes to research their story lines and create their soap opera episodes. Then have each group present its episode, and applaud after each performance. Then ask:

● **What did Samson want from his relationship with Delilah?**

● **What did Delilah want from her relationship with Samson?**

● **After a while, Samson must've known that he couldn't trust Delilah. Why do you think he stayed in a relationship with her and finally told her the secret of his strength?**

● **Why did David and Jonathan have to end their friendship?**

● **How was David and Jonathan's relationship different from Samson and Delilah's?**

Say: **Choosing good friends can help you avoid many disappointments. Samson never should've pursued a relationship with Delilah. But all relationships bring occasional disappointments. Let's see how we can deal with these.**

Make a Commitment

Mending the Breaks

(For this activity, you'll need poster board, markers, and masking tape.)

Before the meeting, prepare several pieces of poster board as illustrated in the margin. Vary the male and female stick-people combinations, and use the following words or phrases as "breaks" in the friendships: "gossip," "jealousy," "changing interests," "lack of time," "bad influence," and "non-Christian lifestyle."

Have kids help you tape up the poster board pictures around the room.

Say: **On these pieces of poster board, you can see some relationships that are beginning to break apart. Some of these breaks can be mended; in other cases, it may be best to let the friendships end.**

For each poster board picture, have kids write ideas about how to handle the relationship's problem on a piece of masking tape and then place the masking tape over the breaking line. If students think ending a relationship is best, have them write advice on the posters about avoiding deeply hurt feelings. Opinions may vary, so some posters may have advice written both on masking tape and on the posters.

When kids are finished, have them explain their suggestions for each relationship.

Say: **You've come up with positive ways to work toward improving troubled relationships. Most relationships are worth mending,**

but it may be best to end a few.

Have each student select the poster board relationship that most closely represents a relationship in his or her life. Have kids form pairs and tell their partners what they'll do to mend or end their breaking relationship. Then have each person tell his or her partner one reason why that person makes a good friend.

Closing

Wild Card

(For this activity, you'll need pens and index cards.)

Pass out a pen and an index card to each student. Say: **On your index card, write down any whole number between one and ten.** Explain that you'll call out specific combinations of numbers and the kids should find others whose cards, together with theirs, make the winning combinations. Before each round announce a different card that will be a "wild card"—able to fill in for any missing number in a combination. Here are a few combinations: three of a kind; four odd numbers; three cards whose total is less than ten; three cards whose total is more than ten; five cards in numerical order.

After several rounds, gather the index cards and have everyone sit down. Ask:

● **Was anyone always able to make the winning combination?**

● **Did anyone never become part of a winning combination?**

Say: **Sometimes we form relationships that seem to be winners. Sometimes, just as your cards didn't always form winning combinations, we form relationships that seem to be losers. And if we have enough wild cards, every combination can be a winner. In relationships, Jesus can be our "wild card"—he can help us form winning relationships. He can help us mend relationships and can comfort us if they end. Let's be sure Jesus is a part of every relationship.**

Close with prayer, thanking God for sending Jesus to help kids build relationships that last.

Soap Stories

As the Stomach Churns:
The Story of Samson and Delilah

CAST:

Samson—The strongest man in the world. Samson was specially chosen by God to deliver the Israelites from the hands of their enemies, the Philistines.

Delilah—A Philistine woman who Samson loves.

Rulers of the Philistines—All the bad guys.

Extras—The hidden Philistines who try to out-muscle Samson.

Read **Judges 16:4-21** to find out what happens. Then create an episode of a soap opera that tells this story as it might happen today.

One Life to Live or Lose:
The Story of David and Jonathan

CAST:

David—A brave young shepherd who loves God and has been chosen by God to be Israel's next king. He's jealous of Saul's current king.

Saul—Israel's current king. He's jealous of David because everyone likes David so much. He's plotting to kill David.

Jonathan—Saul's son. He's in line for the throne. Jonathan and David are best friends even though Jonathan knows David will be king instead of him.

Extras—Dinner guests and servants of the king.

Read **1 Samuel 20:24-42** to find out what happens. Then create an episode of a soap opera that tells this story as it might happen today.

Strength for Failure

"I feel so far from God!"

This is probably not the kind of thing most fifth- and sixth-graders come right out and say. Yet many may be unsure about how to get closer to God—especially when sin gets in the way. By discovering the depth of God's forgiveness and love, kids can come to understand God's unfailing desire to be close to them.

Opening

The Wall

(For this activity, you'll need masking tape.)

Before the meeting, mark the floor with a strip of masking tape approximately ten feet long.

Have kids form two teams. Tell the first team it has two minutes to construct a "human wall" along the masking tape. Tell the team to make the wall as sturdy as it can. If kids need ideas, suggest that they link elbows, hold on to each other's wrists, or cross feet with the people next to them.

When the first team is ready, ask the second team to choose three team members who will try to break the wall while the other team members call out pointers, suggestions, and encouragement. Tell kids that when you say "go," the wall-busting team will have only thirty seconds to accomplish its task. Remind the wall-busters to use caution so they don't knock anyone down or hurt anyone. Call out: **Go!** Then, after thirty seconds, call time. For each wall-buster that crossed to the other side, award the second team ten points.

Have kids switch positions, letting the second team build a wall and the first team choose three wall-busters. Remind the first team to call out pointers, suggestions, and encouragement to its wall-busters. Call out: **Go!** Then, after thirty seconds, call time. Add up the first team's points, and then declare the team with the most points the winner. Then ask:

● **How did it feel to be part of a wall, knowing someone was going to try to knock it down?**

● How was making a wall similar to your relationship with God sometimes?

● How did it feel to be a wall-buster? Explain.

● How was trying to break through the wall similar to your relationship with God sometimes?

● Do you think you're a better wall-maker or wall-buster? Explain.

Say: **We build different kinds of walls in our lives. Sometimes we build walls between us and God. Today we're going to talk about getting through these walls.**

Reflection and Application
Far From God

Have kids form a circle so each person's right shoulder faces the center. Stand in the center of the circle, and instruct students to move in as closely as possible.

Say: **When a person first becomes a Christian, he or she usually feels really close to God. Let's imagine that this ring you've formed represents God. Each of you are as close as you can get. I'm going to read some situations. Follow the instructions as they apply to you.**

Read these instructions slowly:

● **If you fought with anyone this week, take a step away from the center.**

● **If you read your Bible every day this week, take one step closer to the center.**

● **If you talked about someone behind his or her back this week, take a step away from the center.**

● **If you prayed at least three times this week, take a step closer to the center.**

● **If you talked about your faith with a friend this week, move one step closer to the center.**

● **If you didn't, take a step away from the center.**

Say: **Notice how close to the center or how far from the center you are.** Gather everyone together again, and ask:

● **How did you feel as you admitted you had done something to move you away from God? Explain.**

● **How did you feel as you recognized you had done something to bring you closer to God? Explain.**

● **Did this experience mirror your relationship with God in real life? Why or why not?**

● **What are some other things that make you feel far from God? close to God?**

Say: **We may face a lot of things in life that threaten to come between us and God. Even Peter, one of Jesus' close friends, had problems staying close to Jesus. Let's see what we can learn from Peter's situation.**

The Bible Experience

Nightly News Report

(For this activity, you'll need Bibles, paper, and pencils.)

Have kids form two groups. Provide each group with a Bible, paper, and pencil. Ask the first group to look up Mark 14:29-31, 66-72, and the second group to look up John 21:15-17.

Tell each group to read its passage and prepare a news report about what happened. Give the groups these reporting rules:

1. The information must be accurate.

2. Every group member must be involved in reporting the story.

3. Both groups must present their reports as though they were at the scenes of the stories.

Allow groups a few minutes to prepare; then have the first group present its report. After the report, applaud the group's effort. Then ask everyone:

● **How do you think Peter felt when he realized what he'd done?**

● **Do you think it was harder for Peter to follow Christ after this event? Why or why not?**

● **Have you felt like Peter did? Explain.**

● **How did you respond to God in that situation?**

Say: **In Peter's case, the way Peter dealt with God wasn't nearly as important as the way God dealt with Peter. Let's have our second report now.**

After the second report, applaud the group's effort. Then ask:

● **How did Jesus respond to Peter's sin?**

● **How do you think Peter felt when Jesus asked him the same question three times?**

● **Have you felt like Peter did then? Explain.**

● **What does Jesus' response to Peter's sin tell us about how God responds to us when we feel like we've disappointed him?**

Say: **Peter went on to be a great leader of the church. The difficulties in his relationship with God made him a stronger Christian. The difficulties we face in our relationship with God can ultimately make us stronger Christians, too.**

Make a Commitment

Let's Get Together

(For this activity, you'll need copies of the "Let's Get Together" handouts on page 29 and pencils.)

Say: **The difficulties we face in our relationship with God can only bring us closer to God if we understand our part in those difficulties. So let's think about the types of things that cause difficulties in our relationship with God.** Have kids get into trios to discuss the following questions:

● **Have you done things that might disappoint God? Explain.**

● **What kinds of things in your everyday life come between you and God?**

● **When something has come between you and God, what do you think you could do to draw closer to God?**

● **What are some ways you can please God in your everyday life?**

● **What are some ways you can draw closer to God every day?**

Say: **Spending time with God every day really helps us work through those difficult times. Spending time with God helps us get closer to him. Let's see how we might do that.**

Distribute a photocopy of the "Let's Get Together" handout (p. 29) and a pencil to each student. Instruct kids to complete the handouts on their own. When kids are finished, have a few volunteers share what they wrote.

Say: **Take your commitment letters home with you, and use them as a guide when you have your next get-together with God.**

Closing

I Blew It

(For this activity, you'll need balloons.)

Give each person a balloon to inflate, and tell kids to hold their balloons closed without tying them off. Ask kids to think of a time when they "blew it" in their relationship with God.

Say: **Perhaps you've been blowing it a lot lately. Or maybe you just blow it once in a while. Either way, God always forgives us when we ask him to.**

Have a short time of silent prayer so students can ask forgiveness for sins that keep them from God.

Say: **Since God forgives us, let's forgive ourselves, too.**

Have kids let the air out of their balloons as a symbol of God's forgiveness. Then ask kids to get into trios and take turns telling each other one reason they are each valuable to God.

Let's Get Together

Complete this handout on your own.

Dear God,

I know some things have come between you and me. A few of these things are:

I would like to spend more time with you. A good time each day for me is:

It would be helpful if we could meet at the same place each day. A quiet place you can find me is:

When we are together, I'd like to talk to you about:

As I read my Bible, I'll be listening for you to talk to me. I'm looking forward to our next meeting!

I love you,

Section 2:

School Struggles

Cheating Myself

Note:

Before the meeting, place a snack such as cookies or doughnuts in a plain cardboard box, along with a sheet of paper with the following answers written on it:

1. True
2. False
3. False
4. False
5. True

Close the top of the box, and write on the outside, "Supplies: Lesson on Cheating." You'll use this box in two portions of the lesson.

As the pressures to succeed and get good grades weigh upon preteens, the temptation to cheat increases. A young person recently reported, "Cheating is just another way of studying. Almost everyone does it. Those who don't cheat aren't taking advantage of an important part of getting good grades."

But cheating is wrong. Kids need to understand how to beat the urge to cheat and be true to themselves, others, and God. Cheating cheats preteens out of their integrity, which can never be copied from someone else's paper.

Opening
Bad Sales Pitch

Have kids follow you into the church parking lot. If the weather is bad, find a window with a good view of a number of parked cars.

Ask for a few volunteers to be car salespeople. Quietly instruct each volunteer to choose a car to "sell" to the rest of the group. Encourage volunteers to impress their prospective buyers with the good points of their cars and to hide the bad points. Tell one volunteer to lie about the capabilities of the car, and tell another volunteer to only tell the truth about the car.

Then bring the volunteers back to the whole group, and have each take a minute to try to sell a car. Allow group members to ask the salespeople questions. Then return to the classroom, and ask:

● **Which salesperson did you feel most comfortable with?**

● **What gave that particular salesperson credibility?**

● **How did you feel about the way some of the salespeople tried to convince you they were giving you a good deal?**

Ask the salespeople:

● **How did you feel when you were showing a good quality about the car?**

● **How did you feel when you tried to hide a bad quality?**

Say: **Just as some people in this activity tried to sell a car by cheating the customer, students sometimes try to get through school by cheating. But cheating is wrong. Today we'll explore how to overcome the pressure to cheat.**

Reflection and Application

The Cheating Box

(For this activity, you'll need the cardboard box you prepared before the study.)

Set the box you prepared before the lesson on a table in the center of the room.

Say: **For this next activity, I'll need two volunteers to meet with me for a few minutes. While I'm meeting with my volunteers, discuss with each other times you've been tempted to cheat. But don't bother the box on the floor. It contains a special surprise and the answers to some quiz questions you'll be answering later.**

Take your volunteers to a corner of the room as far away as possible from the rest of the group. Explain to the volunteers that you just needed an excuse to give the group a few minutes to think about what's in the box. Huddle with your volunteers for a minute or two to look occupied, and then return to the rest of the group.

Have everyone form a circle around the box. Say: **Before giving you the quiz, I'd like to ask some questions.** Ask:

● **What was your first thought after I asked you not to look in the box?**

● **How did you feel, knowing there were answers in the box that might help you in the class?**

● **Would the temptation to cheat have been greater if you knew the quiz would be graded? Explain.**

● **How was the temptation to cheat like the temptation to cheat in school?**

● **Why do you think people are tempted to cheat?**

Don't show kids the contents of the box. Put it aside until the next activity.

Say: **In Old Testament times, a man named Joseph was tempted to cheat in a different way. But his response to the temptation can help you deal with temptations to cheat at school.**

The Bible Experience

How to Avoid Cheating

(For this activity, you'll need a Bible, paper, pencils, the cardboard box you prepared before the study, a marker, and newsprint.)

● **Note:**
Don't ask kids if they cheated in this activity. Simply have them discuss the temptation to cheat they may have felt and the temptation they feel at school. If you discover that someone—or even the entire class—peeked in the box, don't condemn or criticize kids. Use it as a "teachable moment" to talk about their feelings before and after cheating.

True or False:

1. Potiphar left Joseph in charge of everything.
2. Potiphar's wife asked Joseph to run away with her.
3. Joseph gave in to the request of Potiphar's wife.
4. Potiphar's wife asked Joseph to betray her husband once.
5. Joseph fled from Potiphar's wife without his cloak.

Say: **Listen carefully to the story I'm going to read. In a couple of minutes, we'll have a quiz to see how well you listened.**

Read aloud Genesis 39:6-12; then give each student a sheet of paper and a pencil. Say: **After I read each statement, write on your papers whether it's true or false.** Read aloud the items in the "True or False" box, and have kids write their answers on their papers.

Open the cardboard box, and use the answer sheet you placed there to help kids grade their quizzes. Distribute the special treat to kids while you go over the answers to the quiz. Then ask:

● **How was the temptation Joseph faced like or unlike the temptations you face to cheat?**

● **What might have been the consequences if Joseph had given in to the temptation and had been caught?**

● **What might have happened if Joseph had given in to temptation but wasn't caught?**

Say: **If Joseph had given in to temptation, he could have made temporary gains, but he would have broken the trust of Potiphar—and God. Joseph didn't give in. And he took definite steps to avoid the temptation. Let's take a look at the steps he took and think about how they can help us beat the temptation to cheat.**

Have kids form pairs and tell each other about one time they were tempted to cheat at school. After a couple of minutes, read aloud each of the following steps Joseph took to avoid the temptation to cheat. After you read each step, write it on a sheet of newsprint, and ask partners to talk about how each step applies to them.

1. **Decide to refuse to cheat** (verse 8).
2. **Accept full responsibility for what you do** (verse 8).
3. **Recognize that God is with you** (verse 9).
4. **Avoid flirting with temptation** (verse 10).
5. **Get away, even if you have to leave something behind** (verse 12).

Have everyone form a circle, and ask students to share what they thought of for each step.

Say: **Joseph's five-step plan helped him to avoid cheating, and it can help us to overcome the temptation to cheat, too.**

Make a Commitment

The Best Policy

(For this activity, you'll need a Bible and copies of the "Cheaters Hall of Shame" handout on page 36.)

Say: **Think about times you've been tempted to cheat. Sometimes opportunities to cheat may seem too good to pass up. If you were nominated to the Cheaters Hall of Shame, would you be elected?**

Have kids form pairs, and pass out the "Cheaters Hall of Shame" handouts (p. 36). Have one person in each pair read aloud the "Entrance Requirements" section of the handout. Then have partners discuss one way they'll change to avoid being elected into the Cheaters Hall of Shame.

Say: **If you feel like you've been a member of the Cheaters Hall of Shame for too long, and you want out, here's good news.**

Read aloud 1 John 1:9. Tell kids to take a moment of silence to think about the passage and ask for forgiveness if they feel they need to.

Closing

Don't Cheat Yourself

Have everyone form a circle and stand facing outward. Say: **Close your eyes, and imagine you're in math class taking a test. You can see your friend's paper very clearly from where you sit. Because a good grade is important to you, you decide to copy most of your friend's answers. You know you'll pass the test now.**

Have kids open their eyes but remain facing outward. Ask:

● **How do you feel about cheating on this test?**

● **How could cheating on this test affect you, whether or not you get caught?**

Say: **When we cheat, we cheat ourselves out of knowledge and we separate ourselves from people who don't cheat. Cheating can hurt friends, teachers, and family members.**

Go around the circle and turn kids, one at a time, toward the center. Say: **When we ask God to help us, we can overcome the temptation to cheat and can enjoy honest relationships.**

Have volunteers close with prayer, thanking God for giving us the strength to overcome the temptation to cheat.

Cheaters Hall of Shame

Who should be elected to join the Cheaters Hall of Shame? From the five nominees listed below, you must choose three who you think deserve to be in the Cheaters Hall of Shame—a place for people who are famous for cheating others.

Read the "Entrance Requirements" below. Then read the Scripture references to check out the nominees. Discuss the nominees with your partner, and choose three you'll elect into the Cheaters Hall of Shame. Write your three choices in the space provided.

Entrance Requirements

- Must be a cheater
- Must have tried to get away with something
- Must be sneaky or deceptive
- Must have damaged or hurt others through cheating

Nominees

- Jacob (Genesis 27:1-26)
- The Gibeonites (Joshua 9:3-27)
- Ananias and Sapphira (Acts 5:1-10)
- Laban (Genesis 29:14-30)
- People who pick on the needy (Amos 8:4-6)

And the winners (losers?) are:

1.

2.

3.

Grappling With Grades

Goal:
To see the pros and cons for competing for grades.

Scripture Verses:
Jeremiah 17:7-11; Luke 15:11-19

Parents' expectations and kids' desires to succeed often make school seem like a chess match—or even a backyard brawl. Kids know they're competing with their peers to do well in class, but they sometimes forget that the goal of education is learning—not getting good grades.

Preteens soon discover that competition for grades can be a negative experience. Kids need to understand that good learning is more important than getting good grades.

Opening

Trash-Can Quiz

(For this activity, you'll need trash cans and scrap paper.)

Before class, call one of the schools your kids attend, and get the correct response to each of these quiz questions:

1. What's the enrollment in this school?
2. How many fifth-graders are there?
3. What's the average student-to-teacher ratio?
4. How many classrooms are there in the building?
5. How many days per year are the students to be in school?

To each correct response, add two responses that you make up yourself to create a multiple-choice quiz. Make sure all the "A" responses are the correct answers.

Set out three trash cans, and have kids sit about five feet from the cans. Give kids scrap paper to wad up. Read the quiz questions one at a time, and have kids throw paper wads into trash cans (A, B, or C) to give their responses.

After the quiz, announce that all the "A" answers were correct; then count up the wads of paper in each can. If the number in can A is more than the number in cans B and C combined, joyfully announce that everybody

passed. If can A holds fewer paper wads than cans B and C combined, inform the group that they all failed. Ask:

● **How do you feel about this quiz?**

● **Do you think your grade for this quiz indicates how much you know about school? Explain.**

● **What do you think your grade for this quiz says about you?**

● **What do you think grades in general say about who a person is?**

Say: **Today we're going to talk about grades and about how competing for grades affects the way we act and feel about ourselves.**

Reflection and Application

Grade A Eggheads

(For this activity, you'll need Grade A eggs, a marker, index cards, and pencils.)

Obtain about a dozen Grade A eggs of various shapes, sizes, and shades. Get as wide a variety as you can. Set the eggs out, and number them with a marker.

Give each student an index card and a pencil. Tell kids to study each egg to decide whether it's a Grade A egg and then mark their answers on their cards.

After everyone has graded the eggs, have volunteers explain why they thought some eggs were not up to the Grade A standard. Then ask:

● **How did you decide which eggs were Grade A eggs?**

● **Do you think there's an ideal egg somewhere by which all other eggs are judged?**

Announce that all the eggs are, in fact, Grade A eggs. Then ask:

● **Do you think your grading system for these eggs was valid?**

● **For the eggs that you didn't consider Grade A eggs, how could they prove to you that they are Grade A eggs?**

● **If you changed those eggs' ratings to Grade A, what really would have changed?**

● **How is the way we looked at these eggs like and unlike the way you're graded at school?**

● **Why do you think you're graded in school?**

Say: **Working for grades isn't bad. And it can be healthy to compete for good grades as long as you understand that the grades you make aren't a reflection of how good or bad you are. Grades are important because they help us gauge how much we're learning in school. But making a good grade doesn't make you a good person any more than making a bad grade makes you a bad person.** Ask:

● **How are these eggs like us?**

● **Did this experience tell you anything about yourself? Explain.**

● **Did this experience tell you anything about competing for grades? Explain.**

● **Did this experience tell you anything about cheating? Explain.**

Say: **Like these Grade A eggs, we're each special, even though we're different in many ways. We can apply this truth at school by striving to do our best individually rather than by comparing ourselves with others.**

The Bible Experience

Fun With Francis

(For this activity, you'll need a Bible, copies of the "Famous Failure Finds a Fortune" handout on page 41, paper, and pencils.)

Say: **Now let's see what the Bible has to say about competing for grades.**

Have kids form groups of three, and give each group a photocopy of the "Famous Failure Finds a Fortune" handout (p. 41). Have everyone read the parable in unison. After everyone has read the parable, read aloud Luke 15:11-19. Ask:

● **Why do you think the son wanted to leave his father's house?**

● **How is that like focusing more on grades than on learning?**

● **The prodigal son looked for life apart from his father. How is competing for grades sometimes like looking for life apart from God?**

● **What does this passage tell us about the dangers that can come with living apart from God?**

Read aloud Jeremiah 17:7-11. Give each group a sheet of paper and a pencil, and have groups rewrite this passage in the same style as the handout. When groups are finished, have them read their creations to the class. Then ask:

● **What does this passage say about cheating?**

● **What does this passage say about the person who trusts in God?**

● **How can we trust in God when it comes to our grades?**

Say: **From these Scriptures, we can see that working to get the best grades we can is good—as long as learning is our goal instead of making good grades, and as long as we don't stoop to cheating.**

Make a Commitment

Egg Me On

(For this activity, you'll need plastic eggs and fine-point permanent markers.)

Have everyone form a circle. Give each person a plastic egg and a fine-point permanent marker, and have each student write his or her name and one of the following commitments on the egg.

- I will never cheat to make a better grade.
- I will commit myself to do my best in school.
- I will ask God to help me study as I should.

Tell kids that by writing one of these sentences on their eggs, they're making a commitment to do what they wrote. Have kids rejoin their "Fun With Francis" activity groups and write on each of their group member's egg one thing that makes that person "eggceptional" or "Grade A."

Tell kids to take their eggs home and place them on their desks as reminders of their commitments.

Closing

Making the Grade

(For this activity, you'll need index cards and red pens.)

Give each person an index card and a red pen, and have kids form pairs. Read aloud Jeremiah 17:7-8, and have kids discuss these questions with their partners:

- **Do you think these verses could help you at school?**
- **How well do you think you live out these verses at school?**

Have kids help their partners not only grade themselves on how well they live out the passage at school, but also write down ideas on how to improve living out the passage. Then ask for a few volunteers to share what they wrote.

Have everyone form a circle. Then close with prayer, asking God to help kids trust him more and strive to do their best in school.

Famous Failure Finds a Fortune

(A fun, yet fallible, facsimile of Luke 15)

A farmer famous for his fertile fields, fine flocks, fat farrows, fatlings, and fantastic fortune had two fallible fellows for sons.

Frederick, the first-born, farmed with fanatic fortitude. He frantically fixed fences, furrowed fields, fed fodder to the farrows and fabricated facilities for the farm. From the first flash of light until finally flopping from fatigue, Frederick forged forward for fame and fortune. Frederick forsook fun, friends, and family, forgoing anything frivolous. Frederick frequently fretted about the fainthearted, feeble fatuousness of Francis (son number two) frazzling their fraternal relationship.

Francis was frivolous, free-living, and full of foolhardy faddish ideas. Francis fixated on finding fun, females, and fame. Failure to fulfill family roles frustrated Francis. Francis falsely felt he had fallen from his father's favor. This fallacy facilitated false feelings of failure. Fantasies of a faultless future far from family further fogged his focus. Fluently, he finessed his father into fracturing the family fortune to finance his flight to faraway foreign fields. Though forewarned by his father, Francis still fled Frederick's faultfinding, following fraudulently friendly fellows to festive fairs.

Francis fully forsook and forgot his father's forewarning. From first light till finally flopping from fatigue, Francis frittered his fortune. Frazzled from frivolous frolicking, Francis found himself famished. As fanatically as Frederick had farmed, Francis had fixated on finding friends, fun, and fame from flashy fashions, fast food, and fast living. Famished, far from family, and forsaken by false-hearted, fair-weather friends, Francis found himself feeding filthy farrows for a feeble fee. Fighting faltering fitness, Francis finally figured face-saving was foolhardy. Finding the fortitude to face his failures, Francis focused on finding the familiar fondness of his father. Forsaking false pride and foolish fixations, Francis forgot his fears and found faith in the forbearing and forgiving features of his father.

Since Francis' farewell, his father had focused afar for Francis. Seeing Francis far-off, Francis' father flew to fetch him. Francis' father had folks fetch food, fashionable finery, and a fabulous ring which he fixed on Francis' finger. Fantastic fanfare followed with folks formally fetched to a festive feast featuring fatling's flank, fried fish, fresh fruit, and fancy fiddling.

When Frederick found out about Francis' fortune, he fumed into a fierce fit. Feeling no fondness for Francis and fearing for his own fortune, he fluctuated between frigid frowning and fiery flare-ups. Focusing on Francis' failures, Frederick fussed with his forbearing and forgiving father. Fanatic fixation on fortune and fame flawed Frederick's focus; thus his faith famished. A facade of fanciful fortitude fastened Frederick to frivolous, foolhardy, and fundamentally fatal false pride, forcing him to forsake the father's fondness.

School Stress

Bombarded with school activities, social concerns, and home responsibilities, preteens are subject to ever-increasing stress. Many kids this age are becoming more and more familiar with frazzled nerves and muscles stretched more tightly than bowstrings.

Many preteens will try to hide it if they're feeling the suffocating pressures of stress, though. Kids need to understand that it's OK to feel the bite of tension, even in situations that others seem to take in stride.

Opening

Unscrambling Scramble

(For this activity, you'll need pencils and index cards.)

Have kids form five (or fewer) small groups, and give each student a pencil. Tell kids you're going to give them instructions written on index cards. Group members must all begin to do what's instructed as soon as they get the card, but they must be silent. Tell them that the instructions are printed in plain English letters, so following the instructions in silence shouldn't be too hard. Hand each group an index card with one of the scrambled instructions below. Then say: **Go!**

Group 1: od a eltabl

Group 2: cta elki serohs

Group 3: dnast yb arsich

Group 4: olok yalerl trseseds

Group 5: yalp ophtocshc

(For your benefit, the answers are as follows: Group 1—Do a ballet; Group 2—Act like horses; Group 3—Stand by chairs; Group 4—Look really stressed; Group 5—Play Hopscotch.)

Build stress into this exercise by enforcing the "no talking" rule. However, when one student unscrambles the message, he or she must immediately try to persuade the others—in silence, with hand motions—to do the activity.

After all the groups have deciphered and followed their instructions, call everyone together and ask:

- **Did this game make you feel stressed? Why or why not?**

- **How was the stress in this game like or unlike the stress you face in real life?**

Say: **Sometimes it's tough to know what's expected of us. We try to figure it out, but we seem to keep getting it wrong. Today we'll explore why some situations cause stress and what we can do about them.**

Reflection and Application

Hurry Up and Wait

(For this activity, you'll need pencils and index cards.)

Before this activity, write down the following math problem on an index card for each student:

346

minus 12

divided by 2

plus 14

times 3

plus 4

minus 22

divided by 3

divided by 2

times 12

equals_____

Ask kids to spread around the room. Then tell them each person is going to receive an index card with instructions to perform a simple, yet drawn-out, arithmetic problem. Explain that they'll need to work on their own—without talking to others—to complete the problem in thirty seconds. When they figure out an answer, they must show it to you. If it's correct, they can sit quietly. If it's incorrect, they must try again. (The correct answer is 1,050.)

Pass out the index cards and pencils, and then say: **Go!** As kids are working, call out the time remaining in five-second intervals. After thirty seconds, call time, and applaud everyone's hard work. Then ask:

- **What was your reaction when I gave you the math problem?**

- **What was your reaction when I told you about the thirty-second time limit?**

- **As the amount of time remaining decreased, did your feelings change? Explain.**

- **How was the stress you felt during this exercise like and unlike the stress you feel in real life?**

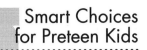

● **What stressful situations do you and your friends face?**

● **How do you deal with that stress?**

Say: **Since each of us is different, we don't all consider the same situations stressful. Nor do we all react with the same "symptoms" of stress. However we react to stress, we can all learn how to deal with our stress in positive, Christlike ways.**

The Bible Experience

Stressed-Out Prophet

(For this activity, you'll need Bibles, newsprint, a marker, and tape.)

Say: **Let's take a look at a stressed-out biblical character to see how God helped him deal with stress.**

Have kids open their Bibles to 1 Kings 19:1-6, and ask a volunteer to read the passage aloud. Say: **Here's an example of a guy who was really sweating it out! Elijah, one of God's prophets, had challenged the prophets of the false God Baal to a fiery duel. The false prophets' God had failed to perform, and Elijah had won the duel. Then the queen of those false prophets had vowed to kill Elijah. He was running for his life.**

Have kids form groups of three to read the passage again. Write the following questions on newsprint, and tape the newsprint to a wall so kids can discuss the questions in their groups.

● How do you think Elijah was feeling?

● What did Elijah want to do to relieve his stress?

● What did God tell Elijah to do to deal with his stress?

● What can you learn from Elijah's experience?

After groups have finished their discussions, read aloud this stressful situation: **Elliot felt like a real loser. He had passed all his history exams during the semester and had received high praise from his parents. Then disaster hit: He really bombed the final exam. How could he face his parents after promising to bring up his grades? Now what?**

Write the following questions on newsprint, and tape the newsprint to a wall so kids can discuss the questions in their groups:

● How is Elliot's situation like or unlike Elijah's?

● What would you suggest that Elliot do to start relieving his stress?

● What role can God play in helping Elliot deal with this situation?

● What role can God play in helping you deal with your stressful situations?

Read aloud Matthew 11:28-30. Say: **God cares about our stressful** situations. He made Elijah rest and eat when Elijah had completely given up. And when we bring our stress to God, he will care for us, too.

Make a Commitment

Who Ya Gonna Call?

(For this activity, you'll need a Bible, paper, and pencils.)

Ask a volunteer to read aloud Matthew 11:28-30 again. Say: **Jesus experienced all kinds of pressures here on earth, so he understands human stress. He says that with him, we can find rest. Have you tried going to Jesus for "rest for your souls"?**

Have kids form pairs, and hand out paper and pencils. Invite kids to commit to praying with their partners on the phone at a certain time every day this week. Then have students tell their partners how they have been "stress-busters" in their lives. For example, someone might say that his or her partner's smile is cheering.

Encourage kids to commit to being regular stress-busters for one another by calling on Christ together and by calling on one another for prayer when they need it.

Closing

Future Fret

(For this activity, you'll need paper and pencils.)

Distribute paper and pencils, and tell kids to make a quick calendar of the week ahead, filling in all the activities they'll be doing. Tell kids to put stars next to the activities they're not looking forward to doing.

Ask: **Disliking what you have to do can add a lot of stress to your week. What one thing are you least looking forward to?**

After kids share, ask them to place their calendars in their Bibles (now or at home) next to Philippians 4:6-7. Ask kids to read this passage during the week and offer their difficulties to the Lord as the Apostle Paul did.

Close with prayer, thanking God for helping kids deal with stress.

Sports: Winning Isn't Everything

Sports are an important part of many preteens' lives. For many kids, sports give them a chance to succeed. And participating in sports can help kids learn about perseverance, teamwork, and motivation.

When kids compete, they want to win. But if their focus is on winning above everything else, the lessons change. Kids may learn to win at any cost, and they may learn that if they don't win, they're truly "losers."

Kids need to understand that healthy competition is less about winning and more about playing. Learning that lesson will make kids winners for life.

Opening

Scavenger Hunt

(For this activity, you'll need tape, newsprint, a marker, and miscellaneous items described below.)

Tape a sheet of newsprint to the wall. On the sheet of newsprint, create a list of items that can be found in or near your meeting room. Have kids form teams of three, and give teams five minutes to find all the items you've listed. After five minutes, call kids back together. Have kids display the items they found, and declare the team with the most items the winner. Ask:

● **As you were searching for the items, how important was it for your team to win? Explain.**

● **As everyone was displaying the items they'd found, did your feelings change? Explain.**

● **If you really wanted to win, why was winning important to you?**

● **If you really didn't care about winning, why wasn't winning important to you?**

● **In our society, why do you think winning is so important?**

Say: **Today we're going to explore what makes us want to compete and win, especially in sports. We'll also look at how our faith affects the way we react to competition.**

Reflection and Application
••••••••••••••••••••••••••••••••••••
Boasting Contest

(For this activity, you'll need paper, tape, newsprint, and a marker.)

Tell kids they're going to play a boasting game that's similar to Mother, May I? Choose one student to be the judge, and have the rest of the group stand in a line at one end of the room. Give each student a sheet of paper to roll into a megaphone shape.

Tape a sheet of newsprint to the wall. On the newsprint, write these open-ended sentences:

● Everyone wishes they were me because…
● I'm better than others because…
● I'm so great because…
● Well, I don't like to brag, but…

Say: **The object of the game is to reach the judge. Only the judge can give you permission to move ahead, and he** (or she) **will decide who can move based on how well you boast about yourself. Use the open-ended sentences on the newsprint to help you think of things to boast about. Remember, the goal is to get the judge's attention so he** (or she) **will tell you to move ahead. The first person to reach the judge will become the judge for the second round.**

Tell the judge to let students move toward him or her by giving commands such as…

● Judge says, "Take two giant steps forward,"
● Judge says, "Take three baby steps forward,"
● Judge says, "Take two bunny hops forward," or
● Judge says, "Take four one-legged hops forward."

Play two or three rounds of the game, and then call everyone together. Ask:

● **How did you feel, boasting about yourself?**

● **How is participation in sports like or unlike this boasting game?**

● **Did you start making things up about yourselves in this game? Why or why not?**

● **If you did start making things up about yourself, how was that like what people do during competition?**

● **How do you think our faith in Christ can or should affect the way we deal with competition?**

Say: **Competition isn't wrong, but we may need to look at the Bible to see how to compete in a God-pleasing way.**

The Bible Experience

Bible Balloon Banter

(For this activity, you'll need Bibles, several large balloons, and a marker.)

Before the lesson, inflate several large balloons and tie them off. Then, on each balloon, write one of the following questions with a marker:

● Read Jeremiah 9:23-24. How would you rephrase this passage to apply to kids your age?

● How could you compete in sports in a way that pleases God?

● How can sports help us rely on God's strength?

● How do sports help or hurt our understanding of who we are?

● Read 2 Corinthians 12:9-10. Why does Paul delight in his weaknesses?

● How can knowing our weaknesses be a great strength?

Have kids sit on the floor, and tell them you're going to toss all the balloons in the air. Say: **Your job is to keep the balloons in the air without letting them touch the floor. Whenever someone lets a balloon touch the floor, he or she must answer the question on that balloon.**

Start the game, and continue until all the questions have been answered.

After the game, read aloud both Scripture passages again. Say: **Many people compete to elevate their status or to receive recognition from others. But for Christians, competition is a way to push ourselves to know God better and to serve him more effectively.**

Make a Commitment

Competition Contract

(For this activity, you'll need copies of the "Competition Contract" handout on page 50 and pencils.)

Have kids form pairs, and give each student a photocopy of the "Competition Contract" handout (p. 50) and a pencil. Say: **Use this handout to explore how your attitudes and actions concerning competition will change based on what you've learned today. You'll need to answer some of the questions with your partner and some of the questions alone.**

Have partners work together on their contracts, filling in how they view competition based on today's lesson.

When pairs are finished, have each person summarize his or her contract to the class. Then ask kids to sign their contracts. As they do, have kids tell their partners one thing they admire about the way that person handles competition.

Encourage kids to take their contracts home and tape them to a closet door as a reminder of their commitment.

Closing

Team Huddle

Have students form a huddle in the middle of the room. Read aloud each of the following statements. After each statement, have kids take one step toward the huddle if they think the statement reflects God's view on competition. Have them take one step away from the huddle if they think the statement reflects the world's view on competition.

Here are the statements:

- **I like to compete because it makes me look good.**
- **Competition helps me improve my abilities.**
- **Competition weeds out the winners in life from the losers.**
- **When I compete, I try to help everyone walk away from the experience feeling good about what we did.**
- **I don't care if others think I'm good or not.**
- **I believe in winning at all costs.**

After reading all the questions, have kids place their hands in a pile in the middle of the circle. Close with prayer, thanking God that, through Christ, we always come out as winners.

Competition Contract

*Complete this contract to help you decide how
you're going to view competition from now on.*

What do you believe about God? We believe...

What do you believe about yourselves? We are...

How might you compete in positive ways? We...

What are the benefits of competing?
In competition, we learn...
In competition, we develop...
In competition, we become...
In competition, we demonstrate...

I believe God created competition so that I could:

I thank God for my ability to:

When I compete, I'll do it for these reasons, and these reasons only:

•
•
•

When I win, I will...

When I lose, I will...

Through competition, I want to learn how to honor God by...

Signed: _____

Succeeding in School

Goal:
To learn self-discipline, good study habits, and how to get along with teachers.

Scripture Verses:
Luke 6:39-40;
Romans 13:1

The word "school" doesn't usually excite preteen kids. In fact, it often scares them. But kids don't have to be afraid of school. With a few tips for good study habits, kids can become confident in their approach to school. And they can get more value from school when they're confident.

Opening

Teaching Blind

(For this activity, you'll need blindfolds and other supplies as determined below.)

Before the lesson, ask a group member to prepare to teach a skill to the class such as knitting, making friendship bracelets, tying unusual knots, making paper airplanes, or writing calligraphy.

Introduce the lesson by telling the group members they'll be learning a new skill. Have the volunteer teacher distribute the supplies (such as knitting needles and yarn) to class members.

When the volunteer is ready to begin teaching, announce that both the teacher and the students will be blindfolded. Hand out blindfolds, and ask everyone to help each other put on the blindfolds. After everyone is blindfolded, have the volunteer teacher begin the demonstration. After a few minutes, call time and have kids remove their blindfolds. Ask:

● **How successful were you in learning this skill? Explain.**

● **How did you feel as you tried to learn this skill?**

● **How is that similar to the way people sometimes feel at school?**

Ask the volunteer teacher:

● **Did you feel you could offer proper help to your students without being able to see what you or they were doing? Explain.**

Ask the students:

● How much confidence did you have in your blindfolded teacher?

Say: **In Luke 6:39, Jesus talks about the danger of a blind student following a blind teacher. This lesson will help you discover how to make the most of school—so you won't feel like you're wearing a blindfold in class.**

Reflection and Application

Study Hall

(For this activity, you'll need copies of the "Elevator of Learning" handout on page 55, the "Exam" handout on page 56, pencils, and equipment with which to play loud music.)

Give each student a photocopy of the "Elevator of Learning" handout (p. 55). Say: **You have three minutes to study this material, and then there'll be an exam. Begin.**

While the kids are studying, give them the worst possible study environment. Play loud music, preferably opera or something else kids won't like. Randomly turn the lights on and off. Be loud and obnoxious, telling jokes or trying to talk with kids about things in the news.

After three minutes, call time and collect the "Elevator of Learning" handouts. The give each student a photocopy of the "Exam" handout (p. 56) and a pencil, and have kids start working on the test. Continue to be disruptive.

Be prepared. Kids may not like your disruptive behavior. If kids react with frustration or anger, help them see how distractions can truly disrupt productive learning times.

After several minutes, call time and have students form a circle. Have volunteers tell how they answered questions on the exam, but don't grade the exams. Ask:

● **Was it easy to study or take the test while I was distracting you? Why or why not?**

● **What things distracted you the most?**

● **How did you feel as you took this test?**

● **How was that like and unlike the way you feel when you take tests at school?**

● **How was this exaggerated study environment like or unlike the place you normally study?**

● **What can you learn from this activity to help you study better for school?**

Say: **If you find you're having difficulty in school, you may not be focusing enough on the schoolwork when you work at home. Finding a quiet, regular study place can improve your effectiveness**

and help you succeed in school.

Take a couple of minutes to discuss the "Elevator of Learning" handout. Ask kids to think about how each step applies to them and how it can help them learn better at school.

The Bible Experience
••

Respecting Teachers

(For this activity, you'll need Bibles, newsprint, tape, and markers.)

This activity helps kids see the value of respecting teachers. You may feel a bit uncomfortable during this activity. That's OK. Tell kids how you feel about the responsibility you have as a teacher. Acknowledge your fears and hopes. Your honesty will help kids understand that teachers are people too.

Have a couple of volunteers take turns pantomiming the actions of teachers they've known at school. Have kids who attend the same school attempt to guess which teacher is being pantomimed. If kids all attend different schools, have kids try to guess the type of class taught by the teacher.

Then have kids form a circle, and ask:

● **How did you feel as people were pantomiming teachers?**

● **Why do students often make fun of their teachers?**

Say: **Although we sometimes jokingly make fun of our teachers, we need to remember that God has given them to us for the purpose of teaching us.**

Read aloud Luke 6:39-40, and then ask:

● **What do these verses say about teachers and students?**

Ask kids to think about a positive lesson they've learned from a teacher. Tape a sheet of newsprint to a wall, and have kids silently go up to the newsprint and use markers to draw a picture or symbol of a positive lesson they've learned from a teacher. After each student has drawn a picture or symbol, ask volunteers to describe what their drawing means.

Read aloud Romans 13:1, and then ask:

● **Why do you think people rebel against authority?**

● **How can we do a better job of showing respect and appreciation for our teachers?**

Say: **This passage reminds us of the importance of respecting authority. We can all be better students if we respect teachers and give them the opportunity to teach us. Respecting your teachers doesn't necessarily mean that you must agree with them, though. You can respect your teachers and disagree with them. Often, some of the best learning comes from honest discussions with your teachers about why they say what they do about a subject.**

Make a Commitment

Accountability Partners

(For this activity, you'll need copies of the "Making the Most of School" handout on page 57.)

Say: **We've discovered a couple of things that will help you make the most of school—choosing a good study environment and respecting the authority of your teachers. But there are many more ways to make the most of school. Choose a partner you'd like to help be successful at school.**

After kids form pairs, give kids each a photocopy of the "Making the Most of School" handout (p. 57). Say: **Using this handout as a guide, decide on at least two things you can do for your partner to help him or her make the most of school.**

After a few minutes, have partners pray together for encouragement to follow through on their commitments. Then have everyone form a circle and share some things they decided to do for their partners. Encourage partners to pray for each other daily for at least a month.

Closing

Fish Story

(For this activity, you'll need a fishing pole—you can use a child's toy or a stick with string—and a picture of a fish.)

Place a fishing pole at one end of the room and a picture of a fish at the other end. Have kids stand in the middle of the room. Say: **Imagine you live alone and have no money. You're always hungry and yet can't afford to buy much more than a loaf of bread. One day, someone offers you either a bucket of fresh fish or a fishing pole** (point out the two items in the room). **Think about which item you'd choose. When I say "go," run and stand next to the item you'd choose.**

Say: **Go!** and then give kids about ten seconds to stand by their choice. Ask kids if they're sure they made the right choice. Then have kids explain why they chose the item they did.

Say: **Learning is much more than memorizing facts, dates, and numbers. True learning is being able to think and apply to life what you know. You can either get a "fish" at school and be hungry later or learn "to fish" and be satisfied.**

Close in prayer, saying: **Thank you, God, for giving us the ability to learn. Direct us as we approach learning every day, and give us the wisdom to make the most of school. In Jesus' name, amen.**

ELEVATOR OF LEARNING

Ride the elevator of learning from the bottom floor to the top.
Ask yourself each question as you explore something new at school.

1. What is it?

Comprehension: Learn the facts about the subject.

2. How can I know more about it?

Exploration: Explore ways to discover more about the subject.

3. How does it work?

Analysis: Dive into the subject and analyze what you've learned about it.

4. How can it work better?

Evaluation: Evaluate the facts and knowledge you've discovered and see how the pieces fit together.

5. What does it mean to me?

Application: Determine how the subject applies to your daily life or what you can learn from the subject.

Exam

1. How many levels of learning are there on the "Elevator of Learning" handout?
   a. 2   b. 4   c. 5   d. 6

2. Match the phrase with the word that describes it.

   ____ What is it?   a. evaluation

   ____ What does it mean to me?   b. exploration

   ____ How does it work?   c. comprehension

   ____ How can I know more about it?   d. application

   ____ How can it work better?   e. analysis

3. List three things the elevator of learning can help you do:

   ●

   ●

   ●

4. The number of times the word "the" appeared on the "Elevator of Learning" handout was
   _____.

5. I think this exam about the elevator of learning is...
   a. the greatest experience of my life.
   b. the toughest test I've ever taken.
   c. an exercise in epistemological dualism.
   d. enough to make me want to take the steps.
   e. all of the above.

6. Write a twenty-word essay comparing the elevator of learning to the "escalator of forgetting":

Making the Most of School

Consider the following ways to help make
the most of your school experience.

- Ask lots of questions in class.

- Study regularly.

- Do all your homework.

- Get plenty of sleep on school nights.

- Go to the library to learn more about school subjects on your own.

- Ask friends what they think about specific topics.

- Form a study group with friends.

- Create a quiet study environment.

- Call up and encourage a friend to keep studying.

- Begin working on projects as soon as they're assigned.

- Don't get over-involved in extracurricular activities.

- Have fun at school.

- Think about how school can benefit you in the future.

- Pray.

Section 3:

Temptation Traps

Goal:
To recognize the deceptive occult.

Scripture Verses:
Matthew 8:28-34;
Luke 4:1-13;
2 Corinthians 11:10-15

The Devil's Playground

Satan uses a powerful tool to draw young people into the occult—deception. He makes himself—and the things he does—look attractive to kids who are searching for meaning and control in an out-of-control world. In order to strip the occult of its power, kids need to understand that Satan tries to deceive while God's truth stands firm.

Opening
Truth in Advertising?

(For this activity, you'll need magazines, scissors, glue, poster board, and markers.)

Set out magazines, scissors, glue, poster board, and markers. Have kids form pairs, and have each pair design an ad for something bad or dangerous that makes the "product" look good. Products could include drugs, poison, hand grenades, nuclear war, or swimming in a pool of alligators. For example, someone could design an ad for drugs that says, "Leave Your Troubles Behind" and pictures a happy person.

After a few minutes, have each pair take a turn displaying and talking about its ad. Then ask:

● **How are these ads like real ads you see on television or in newspapers and magazines? How are they different?**

● **Why do you think bad or harmful things sometimes seem appealing?**

Say: **Sometimes advertisers don't tell you the whole story because they're afraid you won't buy their product if you know the consequences of using it. In the same way, we're often drawn into evil by outwardly attractive benefits that hide terrible consequences.**

60

Reflection and Application

Evil and Good at War

(For this activity, you'll need copies of "The Big Lie" script on page 64.)

Ask for two volunteers to read a short skit. Give them copies of "The Big Lie" script (p. 64). Then have everyone else form two groups: one group to play Jesus and one group to play Satan. Have the groups line up, facing each other. As the volunteers read the skit, have the groups silently act out their parts. Have one volunteer read Satan's part. Have the other volunteer read Jesus' part. Tell the readers to read slowly, pausing to allow the actors to act out the story. Encourage kids to put themselves into their parts. Either you or another student may read the narrator's part.

When the skit is finished, ask:

● **Why were Satan's offers tempting?**

● **How did Jesus know he shouldn't do what Satan asked him to do?**

● **Some people say everyone will sell out for a certain price. What temptations might entice you to follow Satan?**

Say: **Many people are enticed into occult practices because they want power or they want to feel like they belong. But they don't really know what they're getting into. Next we'll look at how Jesus and Satan compare as leaders.**

The Bible Experience

Enemy/Friend Descriptions

(For this activity, you'll need Bibles, paper, pencils, a marker, and newsprint.)

Have kids form three groups, and give each group a Bible, a piece of paper, and a pencil. Then have each group read one of the following Scriptures:

● Matthew 8:28-34
● Luke 4:1-13
● 2 Corinthians 11:10-15

Then ask each group to write—based upon what group members already know—five things that describe Satan or those who follow him—evil, liar, or deceiver, for example. After that, have each group write five things that describe God or those who follow him—loving, kind, or healing, for example.

Label one sheet of newsprint "A Picture of God" and another sheet of newsprint "A Picture of Satan." Have everyone gather back together and

combine the appropriate descriptions on the two sheets of newsprint. Ask:

● **How do these "pictures" compare?**

● **If you'd never heard of Jesus or Satan, who would you choose to follow based on these descriptions? Why?**

● **Which picture describes someone who'd make a good friend? Explain.**

● **Which is better—following someone you'd trust as a friend or following someone you couldn't trust? Explain.**

Say: **Choosing to get involved in the occult is choosing Satan as your leader. But choosing to become a Christian is choosing to follow Jesus.**

Make a Commitment

Grappling Graphics

(For this activity, you'll need copies of the "Light and Dark" handout on page 65, pencils, tape, and a trash can.)

Give each student a pencil and a "Light and Dark" handout (p. 65). Say: **The occult symbols on the right side of your handout each have an explanation. The Christian symbols on the left side of the handout don't have explanations. Look at what each occult symbol signifies, and then try to match the symbol with a Christian symbol that signifies the exact opposite. Draw a line between the two. Then, next to each Christian symbol, write what you think that symbol represents.**

Give kids several minutes to complete their symbols. Then ask:

● **What are some differences between the occult symbols and the Christian symbols?**

● **How does the occult draw on Christian, biblical imagery in its symbols and practices?**

Have each student tear out one Christian symbol and tape it to a notebook, book, or other personal item as a sign of their allegiance to God and his ways. Have kids form a circle around a trash can. Have them, one at a time, throw away the rest of their handouts. As each person throws away the handout, say: **You don't need the occult to feel worthwhile. For God loves you and has given you special qualities.**

Have kids each tell two or three positive qualities about each other.

God's Power Ads

(For this activity, you'll need newsprint, tape, pencils, paper, magazines, scissors, glue, markers, and construction paper.)

Copy the following words on newsprint, and tape the newsprint to a wall.

● vole
● uhtrt
● mdferoe
● fcromto
● yemcr

Pass out paper and pencils to the kids; then say: **Satan's way is to take what's good and twist it into something bad. On "go," begin unscrambling the words. Each word describes a quality of God. Go!**

(The answers are "love," "truth," "freedom," "comfort," and "mercy.")

After kids have unscrambled the words, set out magazines, scissors, glue, markers, and construction paper. Have kids form pairs, and ask each pair to design an ad that illustrates God's power.

After a few minutes, have kids display and talk about their ads. Then close in prayer by thanking God for helping us recognize the deception of the occult.

The Big Lie

Narrator: After Jesus was baptized, God told him to go to the desert to pray and seek God's will for his life. He was there for a very long time—forty days—without any food or friends. He didn't eat a bite the whole time.

One day, Satan sneaked up behind Jesus and tried to scare him, but Jesus wasn't afraid.

Satan: Boo!

Jesus: *(Calmly)* What do you want?

Satan: You're supposed to jump when I do that!

Jesus: What do you want, Satan?

Satan: Don't get steamed at me. You must be cranky because you haven't eaten anything for a while. I'm kind of hungry myself. Hey…I bet you could turn this rock here *(pause)* into a Big Mac. That is, unless what I heard is all a big lie. You do have power don't you?

Jesus: It's written in the Scriptures that man does not live by Big Macs alone. God has given me all I need during my time in the desert. You can go ahead and eat without me.

Satan: Oh never mind. *(Pause.)* Hey, I'll bet you're pretty tired after all this walking around under the scorching sun. I just happen to have a brochure here for a fantastic vacation resort I just bought. It's got hot tubs, waterbeds, tennis courts, a gourmet restaurant—the works! Whadda ya say you stop this God nonsense and sign on to work with me? I'll even give you the resort just for agreeing to work with me.

Jesus: I'd rather sit on that cactus over there. No way—you're a loser. And only losers follow losers.

Satan: So you want to play hardball, huh? Well, let's just see how much this God of yours really cares about you. Why don't you throw yourself off that cliff and see what your God does? He promised in the Bible he wouldn't let you fall and injure yourself. Go ahead, prove he wasn't lying.

Jesus: I don't need to prove God's love for me—I know it. I trust him because he's trustworthy. You, on the other hand, are a snake. Get out of here!

Satan: *(In a hurry)* I'm going already; I'm going.

Light and **Dark**

Match each occult symbol on the right with its opposite Christian symbol on the left. Then write what each Christian symbol represents.

The pentagram is the symbol Satanists stand around when they seek to contact evil spirits or want to be possessed by a demon or Satan.

The symbol of anarchy represents the rejection of all law, discipline, and rules.

The "mark of the beast" or Satan is used as a general symbol of satanic involvement.

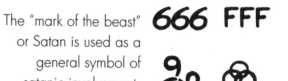

Satan is portrayed in many different ways. Often he's pictured sitting on his self-made throne.

The blood ritual symbol represents human and animal sacrifices.

Goal:
....

To give God—not drugs—control.

Scripture Verses:
....

Psalm 37:4;
Luke 12:15-21;
Ephesians 5:15-18

Dragged Down by Drugs

During the preteen years, many curious kids begin searching for new ways to have fun. A tragic result of this type of experimentation is that too many teenagers seek pleasure from substances that can harm them. Kids need to understand that a relationship with God can be a true source of pleasure—and it's something that'll last a lifetime.

Opening
....

Highs

(For this activity, you'll need magazines, tape, and paper.)

Have kids form teams of no more than five. Give each team magazines, paper, and tape. Have each team search for and tear out pictures depicting "highs"—not only drug-related highs but any kind of good feeling. Then have teams try to build the highest free-standing tower out of paper, with their magazine pictures taped to the tops of their towers.

Allow three minutes for teams to complete their towers. Then applaud the teams. Ask:

● **What's a "high"?**

● **Was it easy or difficult to find magazine pictures depicting highs? Explain.**

● **What kinds of highs did you find?**

● **Why do you think people enjoy those things?**

● **What kinds of feelings do the things in your pictures give people?**

Have kids describe the pictures on their towers and why they consider them to represent highs.

Say: **Today we're going to take a look at different kinds of highs** people pursue. But first let's look at the steps people take to experience a high.

Reflection and Application

Different Highs

(For this activity, you'll need blindfolds, a beach ball or soft plastic ball, and copies of the "Steps" handout on page 70.)

Have kids form two groups. Then blindfold the members of one group. Give each group a beach ball or soft plastic ball. Have each group form a circle and toss its ball back and forth in its circle. Members of the blindfolded group will probably need help finding the ball when someone misses it, but let them struggle to find it by themselves. After a few minutes, call time and ask everyone to form a circle.

Ask the blindfolded group:

● **What was it like to play catch with blindfolds on? Why?**

● **Did you control the activity, or did it control you? Explain.**

● **How is this like or unlike the amount of control people experience when they use drugs?**

Ask the group that wasn't blindfolded:

● **What was it like for you to play catch? Why?**

● **Did you control the activity, or did it control you? Explain.**

Ask everyone:

● **What were the negative aspects of playing catch while blindfolded?**

● **What are some of the negative aspects of being controlled by drugs?**

Say: **Just as the blindfolded group was out of control, people who seek highs from drugs lose control. The highs drugs give are dangerous.**

Have kids form groups of no more than five. Give each group a copy of the "Steps" handout (p. 70). Say: **When someone experiences a high, it's usually because of a choice he or she has made.**

Have groups read their handouts and discuss the following questions:

● **From where do people get their highs?**

● **What makes it easy or difficult to decide whether to go after a high that could be dangerous?**

Say: **People enjoy feeling good, and people think drug highs will make them feel good. Unfortunately, drugs do a lot of damage and don't do anything good. That's why it's important to avoid drugs.**

God has given us a way to enjoy life more—by delighting in him. Let's take a look at what Scripture says about delighting in God instead of drugs.

The Bible Experience

Faith Highs

(For this activity, you'll need Bibles, paper, and pencils.)

Have kids form pairs. Assign each pair one of the following Scriptures: Psalm 37:4; Luke 12:15-21; or Ephesians 5:15-18. Give each pair a Bible, a sheet of paper, and a pencil. Have pairs read their Scripture passages; then have them discuss how the message of their passages can be applied today. For example, partners with Ephesians 5:15-18 might talk about how important it is to choose activities that won't lead to drugs or drinking.

Then give pairs a few minutes to each write a four- or eight-line poem or song describing how the messages in their passages apply to them. Have pairs read aloud their poems or songs for the whole group. Ask:

● **What are the biggest differences between delighting in God and getting high on drugs?**

● **What are some ways we can delight in God?**

● **God wants us to enjoy life, but he doesn't want us to self-destruct. What kinds of highs do you think are OK with God?**

Say: **Many people feel they need a "lift" to make it through tough times. That's when some people turn to drugs or alcohol. What can we do instead to feel good? Let's brainstorm for a few ideas.**

Make a Commitment

Rx for Good Times

(For this activity, you'll need copies of the "Prescription for Life" hand-out on page 71 and pencils.)

Give everyone a few minutes to talk about things Christians can do to feel good and get through tough times. Then have kids form pairs. Give each person a "Prescription for Life" handout (p. 71) and a pencil. Have each student write a prescription for life for his or her partner. Have kids include specific things their partners can do to "feel good" and delight in God at the same time. For example, kids could write, "Go to a Christian concert" or "Ask a friend about God's love."

After five minutes, have kids give their prescriptions to their partners and describe the contents. Then have partners pray for each other, asking God to give them strength to avoid dangerous highs and seek him instead.

High Fives

Have kids form a circle. Say: **God can give us strength to beat the temptation to use drugs. Who needs them? With the Bible's guidance, we can help each other feel good without drugs.**

One at a time, have kids step into the circle and walk around the inside of the circle with their hands in the air to receive high fives from everyone else. As each person goes around the circle, have kids call out positive comments about that person—for example, "You're a great singer," "You have a great smile," or "I'm glad you're my friend." Make sure everyone has a turn in the circle.

Then close with a prayer, celebrating the many good things God has given us to enjoy.

Steps

Below are the steps people often take when considering experiencing a high.
Talk in your groups about places people encounter opportunities for highs.

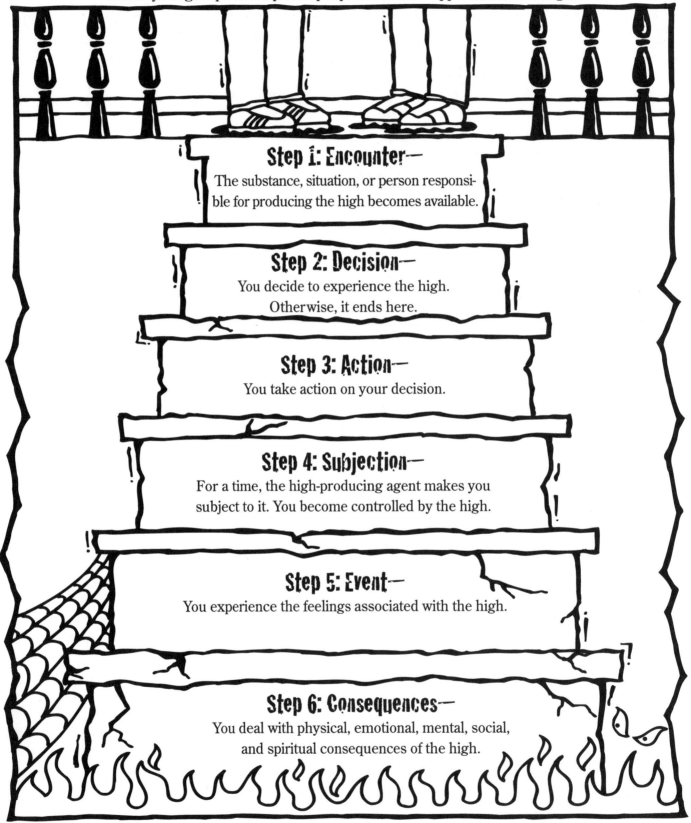

Step 1: Encounter—
The substance, situation, or person responsible for producing the high becomes available.

Step 2: Decision—
You decide to experience the high.
Otherwise, it ends here.

Step 3: Action—
You take action on your decision.

Step 4: Subjection—
For a time, the high-producing agent makes you subject to it. You become controlled by the high.

Step 5: Event—
You experience the feelings associated with the high.

Step 6: Consequences—
You deal with physical, emotional, mental, social, and spiritual consequences of the high.

Prescription for Life

 Write a prescription for your partner's life this week. Include practical alternatives to getting high on drugs. Also include ways your partner can delight in God this week. Be specific in your prescription. For example, if you say, "Read your Bible," be sure to say how often and maybe even suggest Scriptures to read.

Patient's name: _____

Prescribing partner's name: _____

Date: _____

Description of prescription:

Have a Beer?

Many preteens have already had a chance to try alcohol. And kids may be getting strong messages from television, magazine ads, their peers, and even adults that drinking alcohol is acceptable for young people.

Too often, the option to drink has not properly been weighed against the hazards of experimenting with alcohol. Kids need to understand that the reasons for drinking alcohol are weak while God's strength to fight temptation is strong.

Opening

What's Their Line?

(For this activity, you'll need tape, newsprint, and markers.)

Tape a sheet of newsprint to the wall. Have kids form pairs, and give each pair a marker. Have everyone stand with their partners in a line, facing the newsprint. Say: **When I say "go," the pair at the front of the line will need to think of a reason people give for drinking alcohol, run to the newsprint, write the reason on the newsprint, run back to the line, and sit down. Then the next pair must do the same thing. The catch is that no two pairs may write the same reason. If a pair in front of you uses the reason you wanted to write, talk with your partner to think of another reason. Each pair will have fifteen seconds to write a reason.**

If a pair can't think of something in fifteen seconds, have it run to the back of the standing line to think about what to write. Once each pair has written a different reason on the newsprint, have kids face the newsprint and remain seated. Ask:

● **Was it easy or difficult to think of reasons? Explain.**

● **What did this activity tell you about why people drink alcohol?**

● **Do you think these reasons are generally weak or generally strong? Why?**

● **Do you think people who drink for these reasons really** achieve what they're trying to achieve through alcohol? Explain.

 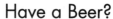 

● **What might be some better ways for people to try to achieve these results?**

● **How would you respond to people who told you they drank because of these reasons?**

● **How would you respond to someone who was trying to convince you to drink based on these reasons?**

Say: **People may cite all kinds of reasons for drinking alcohol. But most people don't find what they're looking for through drinking. In fact, many people find themselves in even worse situations because of drinking. Alcohol is not what it's made out to be. Today we'll talk about the truth behind the glamorous picture some people paint of drinking.**

Reflection and Application

Cover Story

(For this activity, you'll need cooked spaghetti or other noodles, a fancy gift bag, paper, a plain cardboard box, candy, and a plain bag.)

Before class, prepare three containers. Place a small amount of cooked spaghetti or other noodles in a fancy gift bag. Place torn bits of paper in a plain cardboard box. Then place pieces of candy in a plain, wrinkled paper bag. Be sure to have enough candy for each class member.

Display the three containers in the class, but keep their contents hidden. Instruct kids to look at the packaging, and then ask:

● **According to what you see, what might you expect to find in each of these three containers?**

Ask for three volunteers. Assign each volunteer one of the containers. Have the rest of the class call out what they think is in each container.

Have each volunteer take a turn reaching into the container (without looking) and pulling out the contents for everyone to see. Then pass out the candy so everyone gets a piece. Ask:

● **Did anyone guess the exact contents of any of the containers? Why or why not?**

Ask the volunteers:

● **How'd you feel when you discovered what was in your container?**

Ask everyone:

● **How'd you feel when you discovered that the contents of a container weren't what you expected?**

● **Which package best represents the way alcohol is generally presented? Explain.**

● **How is experimenting with alcohol like getting a gift bag with wet noodles?**

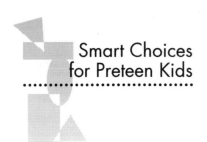

Say: **Sometimes things that initially look good aren't so great once you get into them. Experiences with alcohol are like that for many people.**

Have kids call out negative results of drinking, such as getting sick, getting drunk, or losing control. Ask:

● **With all the negative results of drinking, why is it still so popular?**

Say: **Though popular, drinking can have negative physical side effects. In addition to the physical effects, drinking can get you into legal trouble because it's illegal for kids your age to drink. But what does the Bible say about drinking?**

The Bible Experience

Can of Biblical Advice

(For this activity, you'll need Bibles, paper, markers, tape, and empty pop cans.)

Have kids form groups of no more than four. Give each group a Bible, paper, markers, tape, and an empty pop can. Assign each group one of the following Scriptures: Proverbs 20:1; Isaiah 5:11-12; Romans 14:17-21. Have groups read their passages and discuss what they say about drinking. Then have each group create a cover for its can that includes biblical advice on why drinking alcohol could be bad. For example, a group might write on its can, "Drinking can negatively influence your friends."

Allow about five minutes for groups to read and discuss the passages and complete their messages. Then have each group present its can to the rest of the students and summarize what they learned from the Scripture passages. Ask:

● **How does the advice from Scripture make you feel about drinking?**

● **Would you feel cheated if you followed the Bible's advice about alcohol? Why or why not?**

Say: **The Bible makes clear that people need to handle alcohol with special care; drinking can bring many negative effects. Still, many people take the risk of drinking. Let's examine that risk.**

Make a Commitment

Experimental Odds

(For this activity, you'll need copies of the "Odds" handout on page 76 and pencils.)

Distribute the "Odds" handout (p. 76) and a pencil to each student. Have kids complete their handouts. Then have kids form groups of no more than four to discuss the following questions:

● **Why did you complete the handout the way you did?**

● **What made one risk acceptable and another unacceptable to you?**

● **Would you try any of these experiments a second time if you got away without negative consequences the first time? Why or why not?**

Have groups report back to the whole group; then ask:

● **Is it possible to be hurt in any of these experiments by trying it just once? Explain.**

● **What are the possible results of trying or continuing to experiment with alcohol?**

Say: **You can beat the odds by refusing to experiment with alcohol. If you've already experimented with alcohol, you can still beat the odds by quitting now. We're going to have a moment of silent prayer. During this time, think about your response to the temptation to drink based on all that we've done today. You may want to ask God to help you beat the odds. After a minute, I'll end the prayer.**

Give kids a minute to pray silently; then end by praying: **God, I ask you to give each one of us courage to do what is right in your eyes. Amen.**

Closing

Your Side

(For this activity, you'll need markers, poster board, and tape.)

Have kids form groups of no more than three. Give markers and a sheet of poster board to each group. Have groups take three minutes to create a poster proclaiming the benefits of choosing not to drink. Tape these posters to the wall for everyone to see.

Say: **It's tempting to experiment with alcohol. But as you can see from these posters, it can be beneficial to avoid the temptation. During the coming weeks, support one another, and rely on God's strength to overcome the temptation to drink.**

Leave the posters on the wall of your meeting room to remind kids about what they learned and to motivate them to stay away from alcohol.

Read each of the following descriptions of an experimental activity. Then decide how you'd respond, and fill in the blank accordingly. Be honest with your answers. In a moment, you'll discuss them in a group.

1. A small amount of nitroglycerin, an explosive, is placed in your locker at school. There's a one-in-ten chance of survival if you handle it.

Do you take the **RISK**? _____ Why or why not?

If you take the **RISK** and survive, will you take the **RISK** a second time? _____ Why or why not?

2. You're asked to walk blindfolded across a busy interstate. There's a one-in-five chance that you won't get hit if you try.

Do you take the **RISK**? _____ Why or why not?

If you take the **RISK** and survive, will you take the **RISK** a second time? _____ Why or why not?

3. You have an opportunity to handle a live rattlesnake with your bare hands. There's a one-in-three chance you won't get bitten if you pick it up and put it right back down.

Do you take the **RISK**? _____ Why or why not?

If you take the **RISK** and survive, will you take the **RISK** a second time? _____ Why or why not?

4. At a friend's house, you're offered the opportunity to finish off half a bottle of his parent's whiskey. There's a one-in-five chance you won't get caught. There's a one-in-ten chance you won't get violently sick. There's a one-in-ten chance your body will become addicted to alcohol because of this experimentation.

Do you take the **RISK** _____ Why or why not?

If you take the **RISK** and survive, will you take the **RISK** a second time? _____ Why or why not?

Love Worth Waiting For

Goal:
....
To wait for sex.

Scripture Verses:
....
Ruth 2:8-9, 13-16;
2 Samuel 11:2-17;
Hebrews 13:4

Only a few decades ago, Lucy and Ricky Ricardo couldn't be shown sleeping in the same bed on television. What a drastic change! Today, sexual images permeate movies, television, music, and advertising. These sources tell your kids that sex is fun, sex is cool, and sex is for everyone. The messages are confusing, too: You don't have to love someone to have sex, but if you love someone, you have to have sex.

Kids need to understand that God cares about their relationships, so he wants them to make the right choices about sex. Kids need to see the difference between love and sex to make the right choices in their relationships.

Opening
....

Don't Capture My Flag

(For this activity, you'll need paper and tape.)

Tape a paper "flag" to the back of each student. When you give the starting signal, have kids try to take the flag off of each other's backs without allowing their own flags to be stolen. After a few minutes, call time and see if anyone's flag remains intact. Congratulate kids with flags intact as the winners.

After the game, ask:

● **What was fun about this game?**

● **How was trying to steal other people's flags while protecting your own like "looking out for number one"?**

● **How did you feel when someone stole your flag?**

Say: **In this game, you were looking out for what was best for you even if it wasn't the best thing for someone else. Today we're going to talk about how choosing what is best for ourselves and others relates to love and sex.**

● Note:
During this lesson, be sensitive to the fact that some members of your group may have already become sexually active. Like David and Bathsheba, we have to bear the consequences of our actions, but God still forgives us. Convey God's forgiveness, and reassure students that they can start fresh and treat themselves and their bodies with the respect God intended.

This Bud Is You

(For this activity, you'll need two identical, fresh flowers.)

Show the two identical flowers to the group. Then keep one flower for yourself, and pass the other around so each student can touch it, smell it, and even pull a petal or two from it. Have kids pass the flower until it looks a little bruised or crumpled. Then take the flower back from the students, and hold it beside the fresh one. Ask:

● **Which flower would you rather have? Why?**

● **How did flowers compare to each other before you passed one around? How do they compare now?**

● **How is what happened to this flower** (indicate the crumpled flower) **like what can happen to our sexuality?**

● **If we had cared for this flower, how would we have handled it?**

● **How is the way we treated this flower like having sex with someone you're not married to?**

Say: **A lot of people think of sex as just a physical act. But you can have sex with someone and never love him or her, or you can love someone and never have sex with him or her. Sex wasn't meant to be part of just any relationship, and if people don't think carefully about what's really best for themselves or their partners, they're abusing their relationships. Let's look at some people in the Bible to see why sex shouldn't be part of some relationships.**

The Bible Experience

Do You Love Me?

(For this activity, you'll need Bibles, copies of the "Do You Love Me?" handout on page 80, and pencils.)

Give each student a Bible, a copy of the "Do You Love Me?" handout (p. 80), and a pencil. Have kids work in groups of three or four to complete their handouts.

When groups are finished, gather students together and ask:

● **Which of these couples treated each other like they cared about each other? Explain.**

Read aloud Hebrews 13:4, and ask kids to comment on its meaning. Then say: **Sex is a way to show love, but God has made it clear that it is an expression of love between married people. Boaz made it clear to Ruth that he cared about her without even touching her.** Ask:

● **What are some ways we can show our love to boyfriends or girlfriends without getting physical?**

Say: **It's never too early to commit to keeping our future relationships with boyfriends and girlfriends pure.** Ask:

● **How do you think God wants you to handle your relationships with boyfriends and girlfriends? Why?**

● **Do you think if someone has mishandled a relationship, he or she can become that undamaged, fresh flower again? Why or why not?**

● **How do you think God would respond to that person?**

Say: **Although God approves of sex only between married people, he also has the power to forgive people who've mishandled their relationships. Only God can give those damaged flowers a fresh start in love and in sexuality.**

Give each person a fresh flower. Say: **This flower represents you. Just as you'd care for this flower by looking out for its needs, you can decide now to care about yourself by keeping yourself fresh and new as this flower is.**

Have kids pray silently for a moment, asking God to fix their crumpled flowers and protect their sexuality in the future.

Closing

The Couple to Copy

Say: **Now that we've asked God to fix us, in his eyes we are all beautiful flowers, capable of giving and receiving pure love from him and others.**

Have kids each find a partner, then tell one characteristic of Ruth or Boaz that they see in their partner's life. Close by having partners pray for each other, asking God to protect their sexuality and help them show true love.

Do You Love Me?

Read Ruth 2:8-9, 13-16 and 2 Samuel 11:2-5. Explain to each other, in your own words, what happened in each story.

After each of the following statements, indicate whether you agree or disagree, and explain your answer to your partners.

	Agree	Disagree
1. Boaz treated Ruth with respect.	_____	_____
2. David treated Bathsheba with respect.	_____	_____
3. David had sex with Bathsheba to prove that he loved her.	_____	_____
4. Boaz loved Ruth.	_____	_____
5. Boaz was looking out for himself by helping Ruth.	_____	_____
6. David was concerned about what was best for Bathsheba.	_____	_____
7. It was Bathsheba's fault that David wanted to have sex with her.	_____	_____
8. Bathsheba could have told David no.	_____	_____

Discuss these questions with your partners:

● What is the difference between the way Boaz and Ruth acted and the way David and Bathsheba acted?

Read 2 Samuel 11:6-17.

● Do you think having sex with Bathsheba was worth all the trouble it caused David? Why or why not?
● If you could write a letter to Bathsheba or David that they would read before they met each other, what would you say?

80

Shop 'til You Drop

The Old Testament calls it "coveting." It means to want what others have. Our young people are bombarded by the message that what people possess determines their value. But, what a person owns never seems to be enough!

The Christian faith has exciting news for kids. They don't need designer labels to be of great value as people. God, the ultimate "designer," has already labeled them with the best designer label of all…his!

Opening

Label Me

(For this activity, you'll need copies of the "Label Me" handout on page 85 and pencils.)

Give each student a copy of the "Label Me" handout (p. 85) and a pencil. Instruct kids each to label the clothes, cars, equipment, and accessories with the "best" brand names for each item. When kids finish, have several briefly share which brand names they chose and why. Then ask:

● **What makes something the "best"?**
● **What makes us choose one label or brand over another?**
● **Why do you think some people dress in name brand clothes?**

Say: **Today we're going to begin exploring the way we look at possessions. We'll compare how people measure worth and how God measures it. And we're going to begin with something fun!**

Reflection and Application

All You Can Eat

(For this activity, you'll need several bowls of M&M's candies.)

Bring out several bowls of M&M's candies. If you have six or fewer

kids, give them each a chance to play. If you have more than six kids, divide them into two to four teams and have representatives from each team act as contestants. Encourage the rest of the team members to cheer for their representative.

Introduce the game by saying: **This is a game with only one limit: time. Each contestant will get thirty seconds. In that thirty seconds, you may eat all the M&M's you want. However, you must chew and swallow them one at a time so we can count them. Don't worry about saving any for anyone else. I've got plenty. You can eat as many as you want. We'll have the contestants go one at a time.**

Instruct the teams to count M&M's with you, as the first person eats. When time is up, make a big deal about how many that person was able to eat. Encourage the other contestants to beat that number, telling them they can set a new world record! Let as many contestants play as time allows.

Throughout the activity, keep saying: **Remember you can have as many M&M's as you want!**

When all the contestants have finished, ask:

● **How did you feel while you were trying to stuff in more M&M's?**

● **How did you feel when someone ate even more than you?**

● **Did you feel like you had to eat more than the person before you? Why or why not?**

● **Did you really want more M&M's, or just more than the previous contestants?**

● **How was this experience like we sometimes feel toward getting more possessions?**

Say: **The Bible tells us how God measures value. He doesn't judge us on the basis of what we have, but on whose we are—his. We're important to him regardless of what we own. We need to evaluate ourselves and others on the same grounds.**

The Bible Experience

God's Designer Label

(For this activity, you'll need Bibles, pencils, and paper.)

Have kids form groups of six or fewer. Give groups each a Bible, a sheet of paper, and a pencil. Instruct the groups to read Genesis 1:26-31.

Then say: **In this passage, we can see that God put thought and effort into making men and women uniquely his creation. In your group brainstorm ways God made people unique and valuable: We'll call these things God's "designer labels."**

After two minutes have each group share the labels they came up with. Ask:

● **What things indicate God still places his label on us today?**

● **How would you explain being "created in his image" as a label of God's design?**

● **What are ways we ignore and abuse God's designer label?**

Instruct the groups to read Luke 19:1-10. Ask:

● **What things did Zacchaeus try to replace God's label with?**

Give the groups sixty seconds to come up with as many things as they can. Then ask:

● **How are we sometimes like Zacchaeus?**

● **What can we do to avoid making Zacchaeus' mistake?**

Make a Commitment

I Can

(For this activity, you'll need copies of the "I Can" handouts on page 86 and pencils.)

Say: **People try to convince us we need certain material things to measure up to everyone else. God's message for us is different. We're his children and are highly prized. Owning designer clothing or lots of expensive things doesn't add one bit to our value.**

It's not easy to overcome the world's message in our own minds, but God can help us.

Give kids each a copy of the "I Can" handout (p. 86) and a pencil. Have kids complete their sheets individually.

Say: **Let's make a commitment to improve in the areas we've marked. Sign the bottom of your handout and take it home as a reminder. Each day ask God to help you develop and maintain a proper attitude toward possessions.**

If you want to make your commitment more definite, share it with a friend who can check up on your progress.

Closing

An M&M's Affirmation

(For this activity, you'll need M&M's candies.)

Have kids form circles of six or fewer. Pull out more M&M's candies, and have each person grab a handful.

Say: **Let's think of ways God has put his label on each of us. Think of a positive personality trait the person on your right has. Then hand that person an M&M's candy and complete this sentence: "One way God has labeled you is by making you..." For example, finish the sentence by saying, "friendly," "a good smiler,"**

or "thoughtful."

Then do the same for the next person in the circle. Keep going until each person in your circle has given an M&M's candy to each other person in the circle.

When everyone is finished, close by praying that God will help each person resist the temptation of material things.

LABEL ME

Greg and Lisa, in the picture below, have just returned from a fantastic shopping spree. Label the items they bought with the names of the "best" makers, designers, or brand names that people buy today.

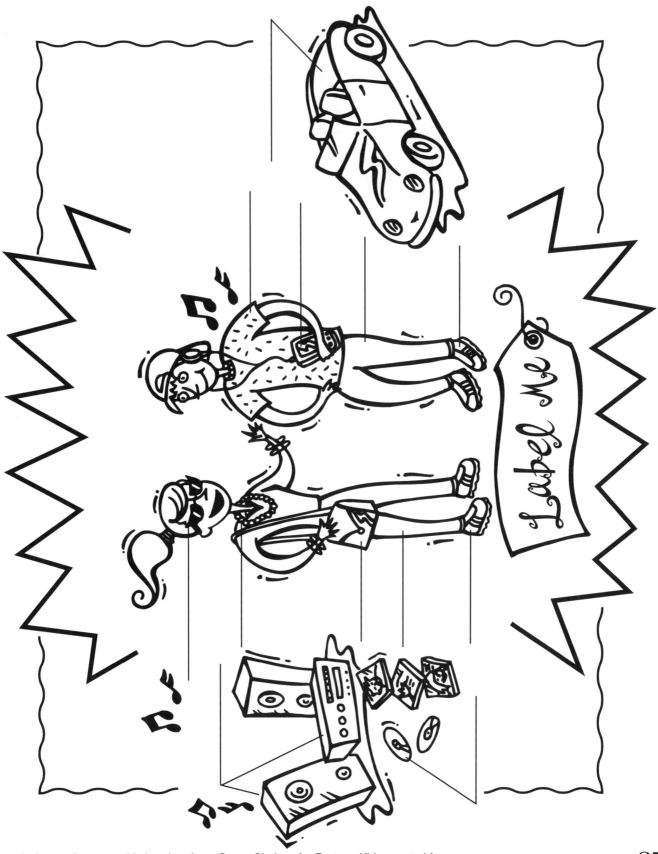

I CAN

If we really believe our relationship with God is what fulfills us, and not what we own or wear, our lives should be affected. We don't need to spend so much time and money working to get material things. We can work on *being* instead of *owning*. And God promises to help us if we ask him to.

On the list below, checkmark the items you already do. Then place a star next to the items you want to start doing.

With God's help...

I can avoid worrying about what my friends have.

I can know when I've got enough.

I can shop anywhere.

I can let God go shopping with me.

I can go without wearing "designer" clothes.

I can ask, "Does this label really make this item worth the cost?"

I can stop pressuring my parents for more.

I can avoid putting others down because of what they have or wear.

I can let God help me make decisions.

I can stop worrying about what others think of my clothes.

Signed,

86

Section 4:

The World Around Me

AIDS: Worldwide Epidemic

Preteens may feel like they're invulnerable to AIDS and other diseases. They may not understand how to relate to people who have AIDS or some other serious illness. Yet they hold within them the compassion for the sick that only the young can have. They need to learn how to share that compassion.

Opening
Wall of Fire

(For this activity, you'll need a rope, chairs, newsprint, and markers.)

Before this activity, you'll need to create two "walls of fire." To make a wall of fire, set up two stacks of chairs, and tie a rope about four feet high between the two stacks. Draw flames on a sheet of newsprint, and hang the newsprint from the rope.

Have students form two teams, and tell each team to stand in front of one of the walls of fire.

Say: **We're going to start off today with a game. Imagine your team is in a burning building. In order to escape, your team members must all cross over the wall of fire. You can't touch the wall or go around or under it; you can only go over it. The first team to get all of their team members over the wall wins. If anyone touches the wall, the team has to start over. Good luck. Go!**

Allow students time to cross over the wall. Encourage students to work together and to work quickly.

When the game is finished, ask:

● **What were you thinking as you tried to cross the wall of fire?**

● **What did your team discover to be the most effective way to go over the wall?**

Say: **Many people face an entirely different kind of obstacle. They face life with a disease such as AIDS or cancer. Simply making it to the next day is a victory. Unfortunately, most of these people don't get the benefit of a team as you did to get over the walls of fire. They must often face their obstacles alone.** Ask:

● **How would you react if you found out you had AIDS or some other serious disease?**

Say: **Today we're going to talk about the problem of disease in our world.**

Reflection and Application

Yes, No, Maybe So

Tell kids that one side of the room is the "absolutely" side and the other side is the "no way" side. Then say: **For this activity, I need everyone to stand. I'll read a statement, and then you'll have fifteen seconds to decide whether you agree or disagree with the statement. If you agree, stand in the "absolutely" section. If you disagree, stand in the "no way" section. Be ready to defend your decision. No one can stand in the middle. You must either agree or disagree.**

Begin reading the "Yes, No, Maybe So" list in the margin. Read each item one at a time, and allow the kids a few seconds to move to their appropriate areas. After the kids have decided where they'll stand, encourage several students from each group to explain why they agree or disagree. Use kids' discussion to ask deeper, probing questions without embarrassing anyone.

If all the kids migrate to one section and leave the other section empty, select a few students to play "devil's advocate" and support the other viewpoint.

After kids have responded to all the statements, ask:

● **What was difficult about this exercise?**

● **How did you feel during the activity?**

● **How did your feelings during this activity reflect how you feel about these issues in real life?**

● **What do you think would be the hardest thing about having AIDS or some other serious disease?**

● **How would you react if your best friend told you he or she had AIDS?**

Say: **Let's see if we can discover how God would react to someone who had a serious disease.**

Yes, No, Maybe So

✔ Kids our age are not really at risk of catching AIDS.

✔ AIDS is one of God's punishments.

✔ A person with AIDS should be treated differently from how a person with cancer is treated.

✔ I would be uncomfortable if an AIDS-infected person went to my school.

✔ It can be unsafe to touch a person with AIDS.

✔ Only homosexuals and drug addicts get AIDS.

✔ God would never let me get a disease such as AIDS, cancer, or Alzheimer's.

✔ If I found out that one of my friends had AIDS, I would stop hanging out with him or her as much.

✔ If I found out that one of my friends had cancer, I would stop hanging out with him or her as much.

✔ I don't know how to act around people with serious diseases.

The Bible Experience

Picture This

(For this activity, you'll need Bibles, newsprint, and markers.)

Have kids form groups of six or fewer. Make sure each group has a Bible, a large sheet of newsprint, and several colored markers.

Instruct the groups to read Exodus 3:1-10 and Matthew 8:1-3. Then tell groups to each draw a mural that illustrates God's attitude toward those who are suffering. Allow time for kids to draw, and then have each group explain its mural to the larger group.

After each group has explained its mural, ask:

● **Based on these Scriptures, how do you think God would react to someone who had a serious disease?**

● **What did you think about as you were making your murals?**

● **How does it feel to know that God cares about those who are suffering?**

● **Are your reactions to those who are suffering like or unlike God's reaction? Explain.**

● **Why do you think God would care whether or not people have AIDS or some other disease?**

● **What's difficult about showing compassion to those who are ill?**

Make a Commitment

Heart Doctors

(For this activity, you'll need index cards and pencils.)

Say: **Sometimes being around sick people makes us feel uncomfortable because we don't feel like we can do anything to help. But even if we can't heal people, we can still do something very valuable. We can encourage people. We can help make their struggle more bearable simply by showing compassion as Jesus did.**

Give each student an index card and a pencil to write two or three ways he or she could be an encouragement to someone who's ill. Kids might write, "Visit them in the hospital," "Invite them over for dinner," "Call or write," or "Do something fun with them."

After kids have written two or three things, have volunteers read their ideas aloud to the group. Then say: **You came up with some great ideas!** Ask:

● **Which of these ideas would you enjoy most if you were the one who was sick?**

● **How would you feel if you were sick and some of your friends from this group acted on some of these ideas for you?**

Have kids form a circle, and have each person take the card of the person on his or her right. Tell kids to turn to the right so they each can write on the back of the person to their right. Then have kids write on the card one way that person already shows compassion for people who are hurting—either physically or emotionally. When they're finished, have kids return the cards to their owners.

Say: **Let's make a commitment to each other to do these things so we can be better encouragers.**

Closing

Double-Dose Prayers

Have each person find a partner. Say: **Another important thing we can do to help those who are suffering is to pray for them. Take a few minutes to think about some people you know who are hurting. Then, in your pairs, pray for those people. Also pray for each other to be good encouragers to the hurting people you know. Then pray for people who are dealing with the affliction of AIDS or other diseases.**

Allow the students a few moments to pray in pairs. Then close with a prayer for the whole group. Be sure to thank God for the heart-healing potential that your students have.

A Message of Hope

When Christian kids spend most of their time with other Christians, they may be lulled into believing that everyone is a Christian. Kids may think that there really isn't a pressing need to share Jesus with their friends, their neighbors, and their world. Kids need to understand that their world needs God and that they can be the ones to tell people about him.

Opening

Human Bridges

Say: **We're going to start off today with a game called Human Bridges. The object will be to form a bridge to get your whole team across the room.**

At one end of the room, have kids form teams of five or fewer. Then have each team stand in a single-file line, leaving about three feet of space between each person.

Tell kids that when you say "go," the last person in each line will run back and forth between team members until he or she gets to the front of the line and calls out "Bridge!" Then the next person will go. Teams will continue this process until they've reached the opposite wall.

Make sure everyone understands the instructions, and then call out: **Go!**

After the game, have teams give each other high fives. Then ask:

● **What's your reaction to this game?**

● **How was this game like spreading the message of God to others?**

● **Do you think most people find it easy or difficult to spread the message of God to others? Why?**

Say: **Today we're going to talk more about how we can be "links" between God and the people of our world.**

Finders, Keepers

(For this activity, you'll need blindfolds.)

Choose an area of the room to be "heaven." Make it a place that might be difficult, but not impossible, to get to—under a table or behind a certain person, for example. Don't tell anyone where heaven is.

Next give each student a blindfold, and say: **I have designated a place in this room as heaven. The object of this activity is to see how many of you can find your way to heaven. The catch is that you all must wear your blindfolds, and I'm not telling anyone where heaven is until after the game. Ready? Blindfolds on...Go!**

Allow kids to search for heaven for a few minutes. Be sure to watch out for possible collisions or accidents. After a few minutes, stop the game and see if anyone made it to heaven. Ask:

● **What was it like to look for heaven?**
● **What was difficult about this game?**
● **How was wearing a blindfold like or unlike the non-Christians in our world?**

Ask one or two volunteers from the group to be "missionaries." Designate a new place as heaven, and whisper it to each missionary. Then say: **With your blindfolds on, try to find heaven again. This time, though, I'll let my missionaries leave off their blindfolds.**

Have kids play again, and instruct the missionaries to direct as many people to heaven as they can. Advise the students that once they reach heaven, they can take off their blindfolds and help the missionaries. After a few minutes, stop the game and have everyone remove his or her blindfold. Ask:

● **What was it like to look for heaven this time?**
● **How did our volunteers make a difference?**
● **How is that like or unlike what Christians can do to make a difference in the lives of non-Christians?**
● **How do you think God feels when we don't reach out to non-Christians?**

Say: **Let's take a look at what the Bible says about sharing our faith with others.**

The Bible Experience

Say What?

(For this activity, you'll need Bibles.)

Say: **The Bible is our main source for sharing the good news**

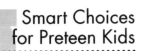

about Jesus. The Bible makes us aware that Jesus loves us, came to earth as a human being, died for our sins, and then rose from the dead. It can be difficult to explain the messages in God's Word to others—especially if those people don't know anything about Jesus. So let's do a little exercise in sharing God's Word.

Have kids form two teams. Assign each team one of the following Scriptures: Matthew 9:37-38 or Matthew 28:18-20. Don't let the teams know what Scripture the other teams have.

Tell the teams they're groups of Christians trying to tell the world about Jesus. They must all communicate their assigned Scripture to the rest of the class. However, Team 1 may use only words that begin with "s," "t," and "a." Team 2 may communicate only by using their hands and facial expressions.

Give the teams a few minutes to discuss how they'll communicate the meaning of their Scriptures in their assigned "languages." Then have each group share its passage.

After both the groups have shared, have them read the actual Scriptures aloud. Then ask:

● **How well did you initially understand the Scripture? Why?**

● **What was easy or difficult about this activity?**

● **How is that like what's easy or difficult about sharing Christ with others?**

● **What do you think it's like for a non-Christian to hear the "language" of Christians?**

● **What can that teach us about sharing our faith with others?**

● **Based on this activity, do you think sharing Christ always means "telling" someone about him? Why or why not?**

● **What else can we learn from these Scriptures about God's attitude toward sharing our faith with others?**

Make a Commitment
···

Ambassador Me

(For this activity, you'll need copies of the "Ambassador Me" handout on page 96 and pencils.)

Say: **When a nation wants to establish a relationship with another nation, it usually sends an ambassador as its representative. God desires to establish a relationship with every person in the world. In order to accomplish this, he wants us to be his ambassadors to the world.**

Give each person a photocopy of the "Ambassador Me" handout (p. 96) and a pencil. Have kids form pairs to complete their handouts, and ask them to be ready to share some of their answers.

After the students are finished, ask a few volunteers to share responses from their handouts. Then ask:

● **How does knowing you're one of God's ambassadors make you feel?**

● **Are there people in your life who you could share your faith with? Explain.**

● **What are some ways you think you could share your faith?**

Say: **It's great to realize that we already share Christ with those around us in many ways. Take your handouts home as reminders of your commitment to share Christ this week.**

Closing

Reach Out

(For this activity, you'll need paper and pencils.)

Have kids stay in pairs. Give each pair a sheet of paper and a pencil. Tell kids to write the words "Reach Out" down the left edge of their papers. Then have kids use the letters in "Reach Out" to create an acrostic of ways to spread God's Word to others. Here's an example:

Run—don't walk—to tell your friends.

Encourage someone to learn about God.

Always be ready to share your faith.

Call someone on the phone.

Hand a friend a Bible.

Open your heart to others.

Unleash the power of prayer.

Take a friend to church.

Allow several pairs to share their acrostics with the group. Then have kids in each pair pray that they'll be able to put into action some of the ideas they came up with.

Ambassador Me

Complete the following as if you're writing a report back to God to let him know how you're doing as his ambassador to the world.

Dear God:

Thanks so much for making me your ambassador to the world. So far I really like:

Some areas in which I could improve my work for you are:

I can see you are helping me when:

Something I would like to accomplish in this next week for you is:

Thanks for everything!

Sincerely,

Ambassador _____
                              Your Name

P.S. My partner says that one way I already share Christ well is:

"We are therefore Christ's ambassadors, as though God were making his appeal through us"
(2 Corinthians 5:20a).

A Polluted Planet

Preteens have heard in school, on TV, and in their communities about the pollution problem. They know the facts, and most kids this age place a high priority on taking care of the earth. What kids may not know is that God cares, too, and can help kids become part of the solution.

Kids need to understand that their faith determines their reaction to the pollution problem. Despite seemingly insurmountable problems, God can help kids make a substantial, positive impact on the environment—one step at a time.

Opening

Pollution Puzzle

(For this activity, you'll need a copy of the "Pollution Problems" handout on page 101, scissors, tape, paper, and pencils.)

Photocopy the "Pollution Problems" handout (p. 101), and cut apart the questions. As kids arrive, tape one question to each person's back. If you have more than seven students, make duplicate copies of the questions. If you have fewer than seven, tape more than one question to each person's back.

Give each person a sheet of paper and a pencil, and tell kids to number their papers from one to seven. Tell kids to go around the room and write on their papers the answer to each numbered question they read on someone's back. After about five minutes, have everyone form a circle. Tell kids that the correct answer for each question is "d." Then ask:

● **What did you discover about the pollution issues facing us?**

● **What's your reaction to learning about these issues?**

Say: **God gave us a wonderful world to live in and take care of, but humans haven't been doing such a great job of taking care of it. Now the pollution problem seems overwhelming. The good news is that you can make a difference.**

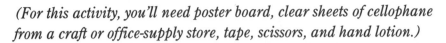

Reflection and Application

I Can't See

(For this activity, you'll need poster board, clear sheets of cellophane from a craft or office-supply store, tape, scissors, and hand lotion.)

Have kids form groups of no more than four. Give each student poster board, cellophane, tape, and scissors to create a pair of glasses (see the picture in the margin). When everyone has made a pair of glasses, smear hand lotion on the lenses of half the pairs of glasses. Be sure to smear enough lotion on the lenses to make them cloudy.

Have kids put on their glasses, and then lead kids around the church or outside. Ask kids to observe the details of the surroundings. After about three minutes, have each student wearing a pair of cloudy glasses switch glasses with someone who has clean glasses. Lead kids around for another three minutes, so kids can observe their surroundings.

Before bringing kids back to the room, ask them to take off their glasses and look at their surroundings.

Return to your room, gather kids around you, and ask:

● **What was it like trying to look through the glasses with the cloudy lenses?**

● **What was it like trying to look through the glasses with the clear lenses?**

● **What was it like when you took off the glasses and looked around?**

● **How is looking at our surroundings through cloudy lenses like living in a smog-filled city?**

● **How would you feel if, because of pollution, the world always looked as though you were seeing through cloudy lenses?**

● **What kinds of things would you be willing to change or sacrifice to help stop pollution?**

● **What do you think God thinks about pollution?**

Say: **As you know, pollution is a big problem in our world. Everyone is affected. Now let's take a look at what God might think about pollution.**

The Bible Experience

Pollution Poem

(For this activity, you'll need a Bible, paper, pencils, a marker, newsprint, and tape.)

Say: **Thankfully, God is bigger than pollution or all the other**

problems in our world. Psalm 98 was written as a special expression of the greatness of God. This Psalm talks about how everything in creation responds to God.

Read aloud Psalm 98, and then ask:
- **What's your reaction to this Psalm?**
- **What image of the world do you get from this Psalm?**
- **Would the writer of this Psalm be able to say those same words today? Why or why not?**

Say: **It's good to hear that God is in control of our world. But God didn't create pollution; we did. And we can celebrate the beauty of God's world today by doing our part to leave the world a cleaner place than we found it.**

Hand out sheets of paper and pencils. Copy the "Poem Outline" from the margin onto a sheet of newsprint, and tape the newsprint to a wall.

Say: **You're each going to create a cinquain** (pronounced "sin-cane") **poem based on the word "pollution." Use the format on the newsprint for your poem.**

If kids want an example, either read aloud the following poem or write it on the newsprint.

Pollution
Not right
We can respond
Must make God weep
Wrong

After kids complete their poems, have everyone read his or her poem. Then tape the poems to a wall, and thank kids for their creativity.

Gather kids in a circle, and read aloud Romans 8:19-22. Ask:
- **What are some ways you think we can help our decaying world heal?**

Say: **Psalm 98 talks about a beautiful world. Pollution destroys that beauty. But each of us can help restore that beauty.**

Commitment
....
Taking a Stand

(For this activity, you'll need copies of the "Pollution Dangers" handout on page 102, pencils, envelopes, stamps, paper, names of your congressional representatives—contact your local library—newsprint, tape, and a marker.)

Give each student a "Pollution Dangers" handout (p. 102); then have kids form groups of no more than three. Give each group a pencil, envelope, stamp, and sheet of paper. Then write the following name and address on a sheet of newsprint and tape it to a wall.

●Poem
●Outline
- **Line 1**—Title
- (a noun, one word)
- **Line 2**—Words that
- describe the title
- (two words)
- **Line 3**—Action
- words or phrase
- about the title
- (three words)
- **Line 4**—Words that
- describe a feeling
- about the title
- (four words)
- **Line 5**—A word that
- refers to the title
- (one word)
- ●————————
- ●————————
- ●————————
- ●————————
- ●————————

99

(Name of senate representative)
U.S. Senate
Washington, D.C. 20510
or
(Name of house representative)
U.S. House of Representatives
Washington, D.C. 20515

Say: **This handout describes some of the pollution problems facing our world. Read the handout in your group. Then compose a letter to one of our congressional representatives about your feelings on world pollution. Be sure to let the representative know what stance you'd like him** (or her) **to take. Then sign and address your letters.**

Allow four minutes for groups to write their letters; then have someone in each group read aloud the group's letter. Have kids share what they like about each group's letter. Collect the letters and mail them before your group meets again.

Have kids brainstorm about things they can do to help limit pollution. After a few minutes of discussion, ask each person to say one thing he or she will commit to doing. For example, someone might say, "I'll walk more instead of having my parents use the car" or "I'll pick up trash on the street when I see it."

Closing

Pollution Sentences

(For this activity, you'll need a pen, paper, and a bag.)

Write the following letters each on a separate sheet of paper: P, O, L, L, U, T, I, O, N. Fold the papers, and place them in a bag. Have kids form a circle. Pass the bag around the circle, and have kids take turns pulling a letter out of the bag.

As each person pulls out a letter, have him or her make up a sentence starting with that letter that says something about fighting pollution. For example, someone might say, "P is for picking up litter." Have kids put their papers back into the bag before passing the bag to the next person.

After everyone has had a turn to say one thing, pass the bag around the circle again. This time, have kids say one-sentence prayers starting with the letters they choose. For example, someone who chose the letter T might say, "Thank you, God, for this beautiful world."

POLLUTION PROBLEMS

Cut apart the following questions.

1. Which one of the following sources of energy produces almost no greenhouse gases or air pollution?

   a. oil   b. coal   c. nuclear   d. solar

- -

2. At what rate are tropical forests being destroyed?

   a. 1 acre per week   b. 1 acre per day   c. 1 acre per minute   d. 1 acre per second

- -

3. How many Americans live in areas where the air has been classified by the Environmental Protection Agency as unsafe?

   a. 100,000   b. 1 million   c. 10 million   d. 100 million

- -

4. How many pounds of inadequately tested chemicals are Americans exposed to?

   a. 600   b. 3,000   c. 15,000   d. 70,000

- -

5. What substance is important for protecting us from the sun but becomes a dangerous pollutant at ground level?

   a. hydrogen   b. methane   c. helium   d. ozone

- -

6. One way to get rid of carbon dioxide pollution is to:

   a. eat lettuce   b. wear special clothing   c. chew more gum   d. plant more trees

- -

7. How many pounds of plastic packaging did Americans throw away in 1993?

   a. 17 million   b. 32 million   c. 3 billion   d. 14 billion

Pollution Dangers

Pollution is a big problem. In your group, read the information below and talk about how it makes you feel. Then decide what you'll say in a letter to your congressional representative about one or more of these problems.

- Scientists predict that up to seventy thousand people in the United States could die prematurely from heart and lung disease worsened by air pollution. Other pollutants such as dioxin gather in waterways, our food supply, and human bloodstreams. These pollutants may cause cancer in animals, including humans.

- Humans add several billion tons of carbon to the atmosphere each year by burning fossil fuels and destroying the forests. This increases the concentration of gases that are responsible for global warming. If the trend continues, the earth's temperatures could raise three to ten degrees by 2050.

- Millions of pounds of toxic chemicals pour into our waterways each year, contaminating wildlife, seafood, and drinking water. In fact, one-half of U.S. lakes and one-third of U.S. rivers are too polluted for safe swimming or fishing; eight thousand beaches have been closed over the past five years because of pollution.

- Much of the toxic waste leaking into ground water from landfills comes from improperly disposed of materials from the average household, such as paint, oven cleaner, bleach, insecticides, motor oil, and antifreeze.

102

Poverty Perils

Goal:
....
To help the poor.

Scripture Verses:
....
Proverbs 21:13;
Matthew 25:31-46

Most of your kids have homes and enough food to eat. In fact, your kids may even take homes and food for granted. Preteens are so busy with their own lives that they may not even realize that people around the world—and probably in your city—are struggling every day for shelter and food.

It's estimated that eight hundred million people don't get enough food to lead a healthy life. As a result, more than fourteen million men, women, and children die from hunger and hunger-related diseases every year. "This figure is equivalent to more than three hundred jumbo jet crashes a day with no survivors," says one researcher.

Kids need to understand that God wants us to have compassion for the poor. And instead of feeling overwhelmed by the world's poverty, kids need to understand that they can do things to help.

Opening

Dream Rooms

(For this activity, you'll need paper and pencils.)

Give each student a sheet of paper and a pencil, and then say: **Let's pretend that you all just received a huge inheritance and so your parents are going to build a dream home for you and your family. You get to design your own room, so you can use this paper to draw a floor plan for your dream room. Remember, money is no object. If you want half of your room to house a gymnasium or a swimming pool, just draw it in. If you want the latest in video or stereo equipment built into your walls, put it in. Think big and have fun!**

Allow the students a few minutes to create their dream rooms. Then ask for several volunteers to share what their rooms would be like. Ask:

● **What was fun about this activity?**

● **What was frustrating about it?**

● **How would it feel to actually have a room like the one you created?**

103

Say: **It's fun to imagine having a big house with all kinds of stuff in it. However, one-third of the people in the world have a simpler fantasy. For them, having a place to sleep and at least one meal a day is a dream come true.**

Listen to these statistics: More than eight hundred million people don't get enough to eat. Forty thousand people—many of them children under age twelve—die *every day* from hunger. One out of eight American kids under age twelve goes without food too often.

Today we're going to talk a little about this problem of hunger and poverty.

Reflection and Application

Munchie Mania

(For this activity, you'll need ten unbreakable items as described below, a bag of fun-size candy bars, and a whistle.)

Have kids form two to four teams of equal sizes. Ask the teams to line up at opposite walls of the room. In the center of the room, put ten different unbreakable items such as a trash can, several Frisbees, a few balls, and a pillow. Assign one item a value of three thousand points, three items a value of one thousand points each, and six items a value of five hundred points each.

Show the teams a bag of fun-size candy bars. Tell the students that the object of the game is to gain enough points to "buy" the bag of candy bars for their team.

Explain that a leader will call out one characteristic such as "people with green eyes" or "everyone wearing red" and then blow a whistle. When the whistle blows, those who match the characteristic called should try to grab as many of the items from the center of the room as possible and take them back to their team's wall. Add up the point values for the items collected per team. The first team to reach twenty thousand points can buy the candy bars.

Say: **There is one catch: inflation. Every two rounds the cost of the candy bars goes up eight thousand points. Ready? Let's play!**

Play several rounds. See if any team is able to get enough points to buy the candy bars. Watch the reactions of the team members each time you raise the price.

After the game ask:

● **What's your reaction to this game?**

● **How might this game be similar to the way a needy person faces life?**

● **How did you feel each time the price of the candy bars went up?**

● **What would you do if your family suddenly found itself** unable to buy food or pay for a place to live?

● How do you feel when you see someone who is homeless or poor?

Say: **Now let's look at what the Bible has to say about poverty.**

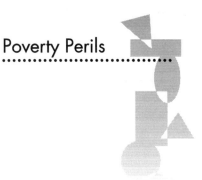

The Bible Experience

Profile of a Goat

(For this activity, you'll need Bibles, copies of the "Profile of a Goat" handout on page 107, and pencils.)

Have kids form groups of five or fewer. Instruct each group to read Proverbs 21:13 and Matthew 25:31-46 and to summarize the theme of these Scriptures in their own words. Ask a few groups to share their summaries, and then ask:

● **Who does God seem to be concerned about in these Scriptures?**

● **Why do you think God feels so strongly about these people?**

● **How do your feelings about these people compare to God's feelings?**

Give each group a photocopy of the "Profile of a Goat" handout (p. 107) and a pencil. Advise groups to reread Matthew 25:31-46 before they complete the handouts.

Give kids a few minutes to complete their handouts, and then ask:

● **What characteristics did you give to the goats? the sheep?**

● **Which do you relate to more: the sheep or the goats? Explain.**

● **How would it feel to be among the sheep on the day of judgment? the goats?**

● **How would you feel if the sheep had helped you?**

● **How would you feel if the goats had ignored you?**

Make a Commitment

Sudden Impact

(For this activity, you'll need newsprint, tape, and a marker.)

Say: **Everyone in the world faces the problem of hunger and poverty. However, some people say that kids your age can't do anything to help; they say you're too young.** Ask:

● **Do you believe people your age are too young to help with a problem as huge as poverty? Why or why not?**

Say: **Big problems like poverty can feel overwhelming, but with God's help, we can do anything. Even a little help can go a long**

way. **Let's see if we can think of ways we can make a difference from right here where we live.**

Tape a sheet of newsprint to a wall. Lead the students in brainstorming about specific ways they can make an impact on hunger and poverty. Some examples might be to sponsor a child in a Third World country, tutor underprivileged children, volunteer at a day care center, and participate in food drives. Encourage kids to be creative, write down every idea, and make sure no idea is singled out as "dumb." After a few minutes of brainstorming, ask:

● **How does it feel to know there are so many things you can do to help?**

● **What is stopping us from doing some of these things?**

Say: **We have the potential to make an impact on our community, country, and world simply by helping those in need. In God's eyes, anything we do to help is really an act of obeying him.** Ask:

● **How does it feel to be able to do God a favor?**

Have kids quickly form pairs and tell their partners one way they can see God working through that person's life.

Closing

Scripture Pictures

(For this activity, you'll need a Bible and several magazines.)

Hand out several magazines. Have a volunteer read aloud Matthew 25:40.

Say: **Tear out three magazine pictures of things you would like to do or give to help the poor.**

Allow the students time to tear out pictures. Then encourage kids to take their pictures home and tape them up in their rooms as reminders to be good "sheep" in God's flock.

Close with a prayer, asking God to help us have giving hearts.

Profile of a Goat

Read Matthew 25:31-46. Then think of ten characteristics of a person who might be classified as a "goat" and ten characteristics of a person who might be classified as a "sheep." Think about what schools they would go to, who their favorite singers could be, and what food they might like most. Have fun!

Goal:
To find peace through God.

Scripture Verses:
Ecclesiastes 3:1-11;
John 14:27;
Philippians 4:5-7

Pursuing Peace

"How can war bring about peace?" "What is peace, anyway?" "How can I be at peace in the middle of a crisis?"

Memories of a recent war or concerns over a dangerous home situation cause preteens to struggle with these questions. And world peace or a peaceful home situation seem impossible to some kids. Kids need to understand how God's peace can comfort them in anxious times and help them bring about lasting peace in the world around them.

Opening

Peace Pictures

(For this activity, you'll need magazines, poster board, scissors, and tape.)

Have kids form groups of no more than four. Give each group a few magazines, a sheet of poster board, scissors, and tape. Tell kids that each group is to create a collage that depicts peace. Encourage kids to use pictures and words that illustrate their understanding of peace.

After about five minutes, call time and have each group present and describe its completed collage. Ask:

● **What were you thinking about as you created your collage?**

● **Was it easy or difficult to create a picture of peace? Explain.**

● **Do you think it's easy or difficult to bring about real peace in the world? Explain.**

Say: **If bringing world peace were as simple as cutting out pictures and placing them on a sheet of poster board, we would have achieved world peace many years ago. But world peace isn't a part of our lives. Whether through wars or through individual acts of conflict, violence and crime continue to bring unrest into our lives. Today we'll explore how God's peace can help us deal with these difficult times.**

The Puzzle of Peace

(For this activity, you'll need a copy of the "Peace Puzzle" handout on page 112, scissors, and jellybeans or another type of colorful candy.)

Have kids form at least four teams of no more than four each. (A team can be one person.) Give each team one section of the "Peace Puzzle" handout (p. 112). If you have more than four teams, give some teams the same handout section.

Place a large supply of jellybeans or other colorful candies in a bowl in the center of the room. Say: **Each team wants a share of the candy in the middle of the room. Most of you want a peaceful solution for dividing the candy, but you each have different methods for arriving at that solution.**

Take three or four minutes with your team to read the instructions and decide how you'll help determine how the candy should be divided. In a few minutes, I'll call "go," and you'll have a few minutes to convince each other that your ideas are best. Be sure to follow the instructions on your handout exactly.

Give kids three or four minutes to read their instructions. Then say: **Go!** and have kids begin negotiating. Allow about four minutes before calling time. Then ask:

● **Has an acceptable solution been discovered? Why or why not?**

● **How did you feel as you tried to solve the "peace puzzle"?**

● **How is this like the way people who try to bring world peace feel?**

● **What made it difficult to come to an agreement on the division of the candy?**

● **Let's assume you were able to solve this problem. What might happen if a six-pack of your favorite soft drink appeared in the center of the room? What would change or stay the same about how each group would handle the situation?**

● **What did you learn about arriving at peaceful solutions to problems?**

Say: **In this simple exercise, you each had a different method for solving the problem. But your solution only works for the immediate situation. Should a new situation occur, such as the six-pack of soft drink we discussed, a new solution would be necessary. And the puzzle of peace would need to be completed all over again.**

Yet, while the peace offered by the world is often only temporary, God's peace is always available. Let's see how they compare.

The Bible Experience

Two Kinds of Peace

(For this activity, you'll need Bibles, cotton balls, a pillow, paper, and a pen.)

Have kids form two groups. Give one group cotton balls and a pillow. Give the other group Bibles and a sheet of paper with the following Scriptures written on it: John 14:27 and Philippians 4:5-7.

Say: **In your group, come up with at least three examples of how the items you've been given can help others be at peace.**

Allow four minutes for groups to brainstorm for ideas. For example, someone in the first group might suggest that the pillow would give people rest when they're tired or hurt. Or someone might suggest that the cotton balls placed in people's ears could give them rest from noise. Someone in the second group might suggest that the Scriptures would bring comfort to people in times of trouble or need.

Have groups share what they discussed, and then ask:

● **What's similar about both groups' ideas? different?**

● **How are the cotton balls and pillow like the kind of peace the world searches for?**

Have someone read aloud John 14:27 and Philippians 4:5-7. Ask:

● **Why do you think the writer says the peace of God transcends all understanding? What does he mean?**

● **How is God's peace different from the kind of peace the world offers?**

● **How would the world be different if everyone sought God's peace instead of "world peace"?**

Say: **When we seek God's peace, our hearts and minds fill up with the assurance that God is always near. Even in the midst of war, where pillows and cotton balls would only muffle the battle sounds, God's peace is with us and able to comfort us.**

Make a Commitment

Peaceful Solutions

(For this activity, you'll need a Bible.)

Have kids form groups of no more than six. Have groups each brainstorm for one situation in which people need to feel God's peace. For example, a group might think about soldiers in the middle of a losing battle or a kid in the middle of a loud fight between his or her parents.

Allow about three minutes for each group to come up with one situation. Then have groups tell the others what their situations are. For each

situation, ask the following questions:
- Who needs to feel peace in this situation? Why?
- How can God's peace help these people?
- How could you reach out to the people who need peace in this situation?

After groups have described their situations, have everyone form a circle. Read aloud Ecclesiastes 3:1-11. Ask:
- What does this passage imply about war and peace?
- How does this passage make you feel?
- What's the most important message we should get from this passage?
- Based on what we've learned in this lesson, what will you do differently when you feel anxiety or concern in a difficult situation?
- What will you do to help others feel God's peace?

Say: **We can't fully understand God's peace. But we can trust that God's peace will carry us through the tough times.**

Closing

Peaceful Ending

(For this activity, you'll need cotton balls.)

Have kids form pairs; then give each person a cotton ball. Say: **In our earlier activity, the cotton ball represented temporary peace the world offers in times of need. But the cotton ball can also represent our concern or love for each other. Think of one thing you appreciate about your partner. Then tell your partner what you appreciate, and give him or her the cotton ball as a symbol of your concern.**

When kids have finished, have everyone form a circle. Have kids hold their cotton balls in their open palms. Going around the circle, have each student say a one-sentence prayer thanking God for his peace and the comforting words of friends.

Encourage kids each to keep their cotton balls as reminders of their friends' love and God's always-available peace.

Peace Puzzle

Copy and cut apart the following sections. Give one to each team.

Section One

You want a peaceful solution to the "candy problem." And you have the answer. With your tremendous math skills, you feel your group is most able to fairly divide the candies so each group gets the same amount.

Of course, for using these skills, you'll need to take twenty candies off the top as payment. But you're confident this is a fair price to pay for everyone getting a good deal.

By the way, you won't accept any other group's suggestions. If they don't go along with your proposal, you'd rather not have anyone get the candy. Don't give in to any other group's proposal.

Section Two

You want a peaceful solution to the "candy problem." And you have the answer. You know colors better than any other group. You know that if you were in charge of dividing the candies, you'd do the best job of dividing them by color so each group could have the same number of each color.

Of course, for coordinating this fair division of the candy, you'll need to take twenty candies off the top as payment. But you're confident this is a fair price to pay for everyone getting a good deal.

By the way, you won't accept any other group's suggestions. If they don't go along with your proposal, you'd rather not have anyone get the candy. Don't give in to any other group's proposal.

Section Three

You don't think a peaceful solution to the "candy problem" is possible. You'd rather fight for the rights to the candy. You don't really want to share it anyway.

Still, you first must listen to each group's idea. And if you really like one of the ideas, you may decide to go along with it.

You know if groups can't agree on a peaceful solution, your military force will win the candy in the war.

Section Four

You want a peaceful solution to the "candy problem." And you're willing to give any good idea an opportunity to work. More than anything else, you don't want to have to fight over the candy. You'd even be willing to give other groups an extra share if they'd just solve the problem in a peaceful manner.